IN
SOME LOST
PLACE

IN
SOME LOST PLACE

PLACE

The first ascent of Nanga Parbat's
MAZENO RIDGE

SANDY ALLAN

Vertebrate Publishing, Sheffield
www.v-publishing.co.uk

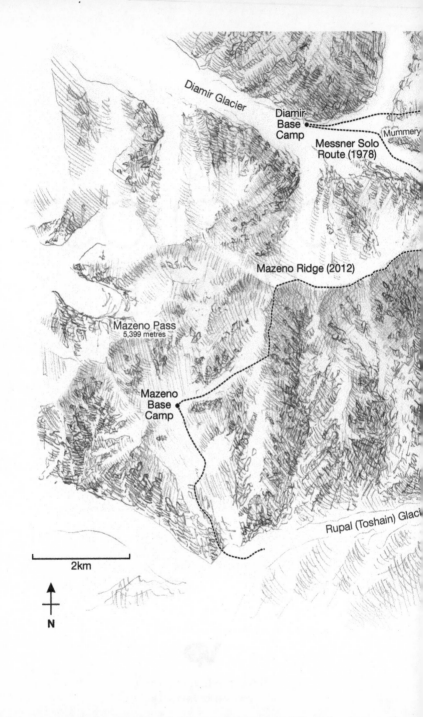

Diamir Glacier

Diamir
Base
Camp

Mummery

Messner Solo
Route (1978)

Mazeno Ridge (2012)

Mazeno Pass
5,399 metres

Mazeno
Base
Camp

Rupal (Toshain) Glaci

2km

N

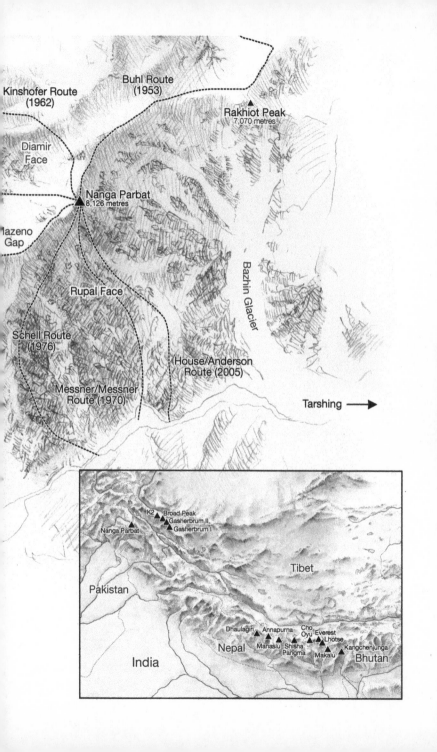

To Hannah, Janis and Cara

Thanks girls!

IN
SOME LOST
PLACE

First published in 2015 by Vertebrate Publishing.
This edition first published in 2020 by Vertebrate Publishing.

VP **Vertebrate Publishing**
Omega Court, 352 Cemetery Road, Sheffield S11 8FT, United Kingdom.
www.v-publishing.co.uk

Cover photo: Lhakpa Nuru Sherpa and Lakpa Zarok Sherpa break trail towards the Mazeno Gap.
Photo: Lhakpa Rangdu Sherpa.

All other photographs as credited. Part 1, Part 2 and Part 3 opening photographs
by Lhakpa Rangdu Sherpa, Cathy O'Dowd and Sandy Allan.

Map illustration copyright © Simon Norris 2015.

This book is a work of non-fiction based on the life, experiences and recollections of Sandy Allan. In some
limited cases the names of people, places, dates and sequences or the detail of events have been
changed solely to protect the privacy of others. The author has stated to the publishers that, except in
such minor respects not affecting the substantial accuracy of the work, the contents of the book are true.

A CIP catalogue record for this book is available from the British Library.

ISBN 978-1-910240-37-3 (Hardback)
ISBN 978-1-912560-80-6 (Paperback)
ISBN 978-1-910240-38-0 (Ebook)
ISBN 978-1-912560-24-0 (Audiobook)

Cover design by Nathan Ryder. Production by Jane Beagley.
Vertebrate Publishing Ltd.
www.v-publishing.co.uk

CONTENTS

PROLOGUE

The howling wind tore into me, pressing my down clothing against my body and driving spindrift into my face, spindrift that stung like needles any skin I'd left exposed. The beam from my head torch punctured the black night, a bright arc in the freezing temperatures. Snatched, foreshortened views through my goggles revealed the vast Rupal Face below me, the longest vertical drop in the world. I was just a dot, alongside five more dots, traversing above a menacing void.

I kicked my crampon front points into the ice as precisely as I could, and balanced delicately on rock ledges. I jammed my mittened hands into snow-encrusted cracks in the rock, or twisted the pick of my ice axe into thinner cracks, torquing the shaft to give me some purchase, or else hooked the pick over a ledge, metal scraping against rock, a noise full of our determination.

Despite the high altitude and hostile winds we were moving efficiently, with the steady progress of a single-minded team. We had left our bivvy tents at one o'clock in the morning and now daylight was starting to break behind the silhouetted mountain horizon. At this moment we reached the first pronounced bump on our way to Nanga Parbat's summit.

Around us, the high summits lit up with the sun's first rays. Above, the rugged profile of an outrageously steep and drawn-out ridge came into view. There was nothing tedious or straightforward here, just continuous technical climbing at extreme high altitude broken up by two steep walls with terraces and ramps of easier angled snow. The towering summit dominated our ambitions, holding a mastery over us, testing our confidence, threatening our hopes. We still had so far to go.

Two of our group, Cathy O'Dowd and Lhakpa Nuru Sherpa, now turned back, a little demoralised, admitting exhaustion and acknowledging defeat. They showed a dispassionate resolution in announcing their decision, a resolution that impressed me, and I wished them well as they began making their way back to camp. I watched them briefly as they headed down and saw at a glance how far we'd come together.

In front of Cathy and Nuru, as they descended, was the apparently endless objective we were attempting – the Mazeno Ridge. It seemed to reach out forever, on and on over a series of eight separate summits, each over 7,000 metres high, stretched out over ten kilometres. It is the longest Himalayan ridge at this altitude yet climbed. Together, the six of us had spent nine days patiently working our way along it, sitting out bad weather, fighting through deep snow and eventually reaching a notch in the ridge below the final climb to the summit – the Mazeno Gap. That meant an average of barely a kilometre a day. For the final, exhausting climb to the top, we faced another three kilometres and 1,300 metres of ascent.

The four of us who remained continued upwards; two separate teams of two with the will to push on and complete this majestic unclimbed ridge in the sky. I was tied in with my old climbing partner Rick Allen. We'd shared plenty of adventures in the past, had even climbed Nanga Parbat together once before and had two lifetimes of experience behind us. What were we doing here, middle-aged men deep into our fifties, faces turned against the inhospitable weather, pushing our bodies to the limit when most of our contemporaries were happily retired?

Our Sherpa friends Zarok and Rangdu took a parallel line up the awkward mixed ground of rock and snow and then we moved in semi-organised unison up a steep and loose rock wall, endeavouring to avoid the occasional loose stones which fell like shrapnel. Dislodged stones crashed into the wall and ricocheted off on new trajectories, whistling through the air as they plummeted.

We continued towards the Merkl Notch and another rock wall which led towards the south summit.

Slowly, so slowly in the thinning air, it became obvious we would not have time to surmount this difficult obstacle and continue our climb up the snow couloirs beyond to reach the ninth-highest summit in the world. Growing despondent and exhausted, there was little option but to turn back. Now it was our turn to face defeat. We had almost touched 8,000 metres, but we were too late, too cold and too worn out to continue.

Standing motionless in our steps, our conversation was amicable, short and realistic; but at some level I felt a little sour – two of us so tempted to push on, two wishing to turn back. Knowing full well that by nightfall we would be exhausted and trapped above 8,000 metres without a stove, food or shelter if we continued, better sense and collective survival instincts prevailed. Zarok and Rangdu announced that they were done. They would go down and would not try again.

Rick and I kept our counsel. We had no ingenious plan. Although steadfast and keen to continue, we had no intention of being martyrs to this climb. As expedition leader, hearing what the two Sherpas said, I simply acknowledged it was probably best to head down, retreat as a unified team and wait to see what the future might bring. We turned around dejected but knowing we had tried. The retreat back to the bivvy site would not be straightforward.

To save time, I suggested a shortcut, traversing an easy snow ramp to a small notch where a vague narrow ledge divided the rock wall we had climbed earlier. Below and above the ledge was a steep cliff. I led down, using my ice pick to hook ledges, my crampons stabbing placements on the snow-encrusted and brittle rock. The others tentatively followed, questioning the wisdom of my route, wondering if my chosen line would get easier or harder.

The ledge continued. On one small but awkward overhanging step, I placed my ice tool above me, torquing the pick and holding tight to the shaft. I lowered my body downwards, trying to place my clumsy high-altitude boot and front points on to a tiny protrusion of rock. From here I hoped to transfer my weight and step down on to a slightly wider ledge, but the torqued pick pulled out from the crack and down I fell, the ragged rock tearing my down trousers. A plume of the finest quality duck down filled the air and gasping with hypoxia I breathed it in, filling my throat with feathers.

Choking, I spat them from my already dehydrated mouth. My legs floundered against the rock as Rick held the rope tight to stop my fall. Regaining composure and breathing more regularly, I led on down the thirty-five-degree traverse, flicking the rope over small rock flakes. If I fell again there was a chance the rope would catch on the flakes, reduce the fall and stop me pulling my partner down the sheer cliff with me. The climbing felt intense and as I cleaned the soft snow off ledges, looking for cracks in which to place my ice axe pick, my tired body buckled with stress. We had now been climbing continuously for fourteen hours: this was our eleventh consecutive day, and ten of those days had been at around 7,000 metres.

Once off the tricky rock ledge, the snow ramp looked steep but straightforward. We carried on traversing for what felt like hours. Tying our ropes together, two abseils brought us through another band of rocks where an easy snow ramp seemed to lead eventually to our bivvy. We stopped, kicked small ledges in the snow and rested, drinking the last water from our bottles. We were exhausted, completely done in, and I was not looking forward to breaking trail ahead. We shared the last of our packed food and partially relaxed.

We talked and joked with each other, and this gave us confidence as we decided to move on. Now it was Zarok's turn in front and he set off almost casually. Stepping forwards in the deep snow I saw Zarok catch his crampon on his boot. He tripped and fell on to the steep snow slope. There was some loose rope lying on the snow between him and Rangdu, and Zarok continued to fall, tobogganing down the slope with ever-increasing speed.

I saw Rangdu stamp his feet and thrust his ice axe into the snow, ready to brace the fall. Then the rope coils ran out and the cord between them pinged tight with Rangdu braced for the strain only to be snatched up and out, flying into space like a champagne cork popping from a bottle.

Rangdu shot off down the slope, overtaking Zarok, with both men sliding upside down and out of control. As they careered downwards, Zarok overtook Rangdu again, as if it were a race. Below them were the steep and violently contorted séracs and icefalls of the Diamir Face. Like torpedoes, both Sherpas followed a deadly trajectory to the rugged edge of the vast ice cliffs below. A few metres further and they would be launched into space and plummet towards the valley floor several thousand metres below. There would be no chance of survival. All Rick and I could do was watch in horror.

PART 1
THE MAGIC BUS

TEAM SPIRIT

Nanga Parbat stands alone. It might be physically close to the great mountains of the Karakoram like K2 and Broad Peak, off to the north-east, but it is in reality the western wall of the Himalaya, the last flourish of a range that extends east in a narrow arc some 2,500 kilometres long to the fringes of China. Nanga Parbat translates from Urdu as 'naked mountain', a name that captures the idea of a peak that rises from the plains in full view. It is the ninth-highest peak in the world, one of the fourteen 8,000-metre peaks and the most westerly. Although the Karakoram peaks are close, its nearest 8,000-metre neighbour in the Himalaya is Dhaulagiri, some 1,400 kilometres further east.

This sense of grand isolation is deepened by Nanga Parbat's incredible topography. The mighty Indus flows round its northern and western flanks at little more than a thousand metres in altitude, carving a deep gorge around the mountain some 7,000 metres below the summit of the peak. Nanga Parbat's Rupal Face is around 4,500 metres high, the highest mountain wall in the world. It's no coincidence that, at the time of writing, only two peaks over 8,000 metres remain to be climbed in winter: K2 and Nanga Parbat.[1] And while K2 lies hidden up the Baltoro Glacier, many days' walk away, it takes just a few hours from the road to reach Nanga Parbat's base camps. Its sheer size and exposure to bad weather has stopped all comers.

So perhaps it's all the more amazing that Nanga Parbat was the first 8,000-metre peak to be attempted – and back in the

[1] The first winter ascent of Nanga Parbat was subsequently made by Simone Moro, Alex Txikon and Ali Sadpara in February 2016.

nineteenth century too. This amazing step into the unknown was taken by Albert Frederick Mummery, one of the leading alpinists of his day and a visionary when it came to both what was possible in the mountains and how his ambitions should be realised, by what Mummery called 'fair means'.

He was born in Kent and as a sickly child might have seemed an unlikely contender to be the first man to climb an eight-thousander, but with his small team of just two others – J. Norman Collie and Geoffrey Hastings – that's precisely what he set out to do in 1895, and in an amazing lightweight style too. Sadly, he perished in the attempt, along with two Gurkha soldiers acting as porters, most probably in an avalanche. There had only been a handful of Himalayan climbing expeditions at this point, and if Mummery was naive and overenthusiastic, his instinct for 'fair means' in the Himalaya has inspired subsequent generations, including Reinhold Messner, the first man to climb all fourteen 8,000-metre peaks.

Those who know the story of Nanga Parbat often describe it as a German mountain, in the sense that it was German climbers who tried again and again to make the first ascent in the 1930s, but unsuccessfully and with a grim loss of life. Great climbers like Willy Merkl and Willo Welzenbach met their ends in a sequence of terrible disasters. In just two expeditions, in 1934 and 1937, twenty-four climbers and Sherpas lost their lives. Altogether, thirty-one men died before Nanga Parbat was finally climbed in 1953 by Hermann Buhl. Seventeen of those men were Sherpas. This sequence of dreadful accidents earned Nanga Parbat the sobering nickname 'killer mountain'.

Even after Hermann Buhl became the first man to reach the top, climbing in a super-lightweight dash that Mummery might have admired, many of the significant new routes done on the peak were German. This was partly because of the obsession of one man – Karl Herrligkoffer. He was the half-brother of Willy Merkl, who led attempts on Nanga Parbat in 1932 and 1934 and perished in a terrible storm that took the lives of three climbers and six Sherpas. Nanga Parbat was consequently Herrligkoffer's obsession. He led eight expeditions there in all, including the 1953 climb when Buhl reached the summit, much against Herrligkoffer's orders. Two more hugely important climbs were made by teams under Herrligkoffer's command: a route up the Diamir Face in 1962 now known as the Kinshofer and the normal line of ascent, and the first ascent of the Rupal Face in 1970, when Reinhold Messner reached the summit with his brother Günther, who died as they descended the Diamir side of the mountain.

With the major faces of Nanga Parbat climbed, there was just one major feature left to climb, one so vast it barely merited consideration. But that's what each new generation of climbers does – considers the impossible, and how it might be achieved. Nanga Parbat's west ridge is more commonly known as the Mazeno. It takes its name from the saddle at its western end – the Mazeno Pass. Most likely, it's derived from the local Shina word *majeno*, meaning 'the middle', or 'between two places', which the pass most definitely is for people living in Astore and Bunar. For centuries immemorial it's been a handy route for bandits sneaking over from Chilas. The ridge itself is vast, around ten kilometres long, a dragon's back with eight separate summits to cross before you arrive at a col known as the Mazeno Gap, just below the final summit pyramid. The highest of those intermediate summits is Mazeno Peak, at 7,120 metres, and just before the Mazeno Gap is a series of awkward, technical pinnacles – a real sting in the tail.

For those who know the Isle of Skye, it's slightly shorter than the Cuillin Ridge, except that most of the Mazeno is at around 7,000 metres and not 3,000 feet. It might be possible to run along the Cuillin, but no one is running anywhere at this altitude yet. The Mazeno is also flanked on either side by huge drops – a real tightrope in the sky – and the only way to escape it is at either end: the Mazeno Pass to the west or the Mazeno Gap to the east, in the lee of the summit. Once you're on it, you either have to retrace your steps or press on. There is no down. The Mazeno is no place to get caught in a storm.

These complications leave climbers in a classic dilemma. On such a long and complex objective you have to choose between carrying enough supplies to keep you going, and not making your rucksack so heavy that you end up moving slowly. This will cost you more time and mean, consequently, that you need more supplies, which in turn makes your rucksack heavier. Snow conditions are also critical. What might be a straightforward slope one day could take four times as long if it's covered with unconsolidated snow. And when you have an objective as big as the Mazeno, all these problems are exponentially bigger.

It's hardly surprising that over the years the Mazeno became one of the great unclimbed challenges for the world's high-altitude climbers. It looked so vast and tempting, but how would they succeed?

First to try was a huge French team of climbers who fixed a lot of rope but only reached a small peak at the start of the ridge. I had no interest in a big, fixed-rope expedition. The real challenge of the Mazeno was to climb it as light as possible. Doug Scott led three expeditions in the 1990s, and on the first of these made some good progress. His team had initially climbed up to the end of the ridge near the Mazeno Gap via the Schell route to leave a stash of gear they could use coming along the ridge. But the climbers were strafed by rockfall and the Russian Valeri Pershin suffered bad injuries. When Doug did get on to the Mazeno Ridge, with Sergey Efimov and Ang Phurba, they made good progress until Ang Phurba called a halt in windy conditions. He too had been injured in the earlier accident and couldn't go on.

Rick Allen and I joined Doug in 1995 for his third try. It was then that the Mazeno first got under my skin. In the early stages of that expedition I climbed with Voytek Kurtyka, the legendary Polish alpinist. When Doug left the expedition, suffering from a severe stomach illness, I felt strangely out of sorts, and eventually left to catch Doug up as I missed him so much. The remaining climbers stuck at it until they reached a spot on the ridge we'd dubbed 'the point of no return' – the spot where it would be easier just to keep going to the Mazeno Gap and descend, if necessary, from there, than it would be to turn back.

Voytek had another go in 1997, but didn't get any further than he had before. The real breakthrough came seven years later when two strong Americans, Steve Swenson and Doug Chabot, raced along the ridge which was in excellent condition, to reach the Mazeno Gap in just four days. When they arrived that summer in the village below the Rupal Face, the locals asked them: 'You trying Doug Scott route? Not possible. Schell route much better.' Steve and Doug had proved them wrong. Yet when they got to the Mazeno Gap, Doug was sick and the weather was deteriorating. They opted to descend the Schell route rather than climb up another 1,200 metres to the summit. Four years later, two experienced German climbers, Luis Stitzinger and Josef Lunger, did pretty much the same thing, taking slightly longer and consequently running out of food and gas at the Mazeno Gap. Twice now, strong, well-acclimatised teams of two had managed to climb the ridge but had not been in good enough shape to carry on to the summit.

Much progress had been made in the thirty-three years since that first attempt on the Mazeno. Clothing and equipment were much better, as were attitudes and knowledge. In addition, weather forecasting was much more reliable. Yet this great beast was still unclimbed. Now, almost twenty years after my first attempt, I was on my way back for another try.

Stepping through the aircraft door at Islamabad airport, a blast of hot air rising off the tarmac hit me in the face. It was 10 June 2012. I had flown in from London with Cathy O'Dowd, and we were through customs in no time, spilling out on to the concourse where Muhammad Ali, our agent and the director of Adventure Pakistan, was waiting to collect us. He led the way with an entourage of airport porters to a four-wheel-drive truck.

I love the early days of an expedition, arriving in South Asia, plunging back into the frenetic pace of city life there. Expeditions are really organised chaos, an exact reflection of life – or at least my life. The noise and chaos of the city were familiar to me, but rush hour hadn't started yet, so the streets were relatively quiet. At the hotel where Rick and the three Sherpas were waiting for us, barriers across the entrance at the top of the drive blocked anyone from getting too close too soon, a protective measure against the terrorist attacks and suicide bombers that have made life in Pakistan so difficult. Police and hotel security guards pored over our passports and glanced over our baggage in the back of the pick-up. Only then were we permitted to drive into the hotel grounds.

Immediately, I spotted a bus parked in a corner of the compound loaded with expedition kitbags. As we'd arranged, Rick had got everything organised for a rapid departure. Inside the hotel Lhakpa Rangdu Sherpa, Lhakpa Nuru Sherpa, Lakpa Zarok Sherpa – the 'three Lhakpas' – and Rick were tucking into breakfast. We hugged and shook hands, and I grabbed a mango juice. It was so great to see them again. The otherwise empty restaurant was suddenly full of the energy of a great new adventure. It felt like years of planning were finally coming together.

Once I had introduced Cathy to the Sherpas, Rick explained everything was ready and we could start our drive up the Karakoram Highway straight away. I told him I wasn't going anywhere without a shower. Cathy disappeared into Rick's room and I used the Sherpas', stepping over the chaos of an abandoned hotel room. An extra mattress lay on the floor, like Tracey Emin's unmade bed, but without the backstory. I found some soap, a used towel and a disposable razor and luxuriated in the feel of warm, clean water on my skin. I knew that in a few days I would be dreaming of a hot shower in a half-decent bathroom and I wasn't about to waste the chance now.

Changing into trekking pants and a T-shirt, I filled my wash kit with the remaining soaps and shampoos and rushed downstairs to where the bags holding all my important high-altitude climbing clothing and equipment were stacked on the lobby floor. Working quickly, I began to rearrange my gear and pulled out my ice tools. My heart sank. They were not at all what I wanted; certainly not the sort of axes you'd want on the climb of a lifetime.

This was largely my own fault. For the last few weeks I'd been working in Australia, helping to set up an industrial rope access division for a Scottish and Australian joint venture. I had been set up in offices in the trendiest part of Perth, with a personal assistant who seemed to know every secret detail of every important business in Western Australia. But the Scottish businessmen I was working for had kept me hanging on in Perth till the last minute. I had planned a week in Chamonix to acclimatise and recover my usual gear, but there had no longer been time for that. Rick reassured me there were adequate ice tools in our Pakistani stash, but, as I now discovered, they were cheap and low-quality knock-offs made in Eastern Europe.

Rick and I have different attitudes to money. I often crack a joke that the British fifty-pence coin has heptagonal edges so you can use a wrench to extract it from Rick's hand. Then again, his sound approach to cash flow has bailed out our expeditions on more than one occasion. My life as an itinerant mountain guide means that I have quite a small income and, while I do also get some interesting work in the rope access industry, the money is soon gone on climbing and helping out my daughters. My father often warned me about fast women and slow horses but I can't have listened too well; a balanced bank account is not something I manage easily, nor, for that matter, is a lasting marriage. While I love being in the mountains, with all their austerity, when I'm in the Chamonix valley I have a tendency towards the luxurious, with a taste for expensive restaurants and vintage wines. I was reminded by one of my pals that my motto used to be that to die in credit was to die in disgrace.

In the 1980s, I went on expeditions with the poet and novelist Andrew Greig, including one to Lhotse Shar near Everest, where he wrote a poem about it in his book *Getting Higher*, called 'Three Above Namche Bazaar':

'Sandy, feeling somewhat queasy,/squatted above Namche,/shat a five-foot worm. My life's/like that, he said as we/laughed and took our photographs,/a thread of consistency/through unconsolidated crap.'[2]

Much of what happens in life can be put down to chance, but even though I think I've had more than my share of good luck, when it comes to the basic rules of mountaineering, I am blessed with a very strong sense of discipline; to do things properly when required, and that includes having the right ice axes for the job.

Still, when we at last loaded my bags on to the bus, I felt a burst of optimism. After years of planning, thinking and dreaming, we were moments away from finally setting off. Cathy had sorted herself out much more quickly and was impatient with me for being so slow. I excused myself for being a man, unable to do several things at once. We said our goodbyes to Ali and climbed aboard to be driven away into the madness of Islamabad's streets. Pakistani music blared from the vehicle's radio, and I helped myself to the drinks from the cooler Ali's people had filled for us. After just an hour and a half in Islamabad, we had, thanks to Ali, Rick and the Sherpas, already started the twenty-four-hour drive along the Karakoram Highway – one of the most amazing roads in the world – bound for the small village of Chilas, an important staging post on the highway.

Known in Pakistan as the KKH, the road is excellent at first, and we sped out of the city. True, we sometimes shrieked in fear as drivers yo-yoed between lanes at high speed without warning,

---

2 *Getting Higher: The complete mountain poems* (Polygon, 2011).

braking dramatically and swerving to avoid overloaded trucks that wallowed like whales, or the three-wheel taxis and donkey carts. But after a few hours of this, the KKH narrowed to two lanes and we were out in the country, dodging massive potholes.

Every time we paused in the road, a horde of adults and kids tried to sell us drinks, snacks, cheap plastic necklaces and pretty much anything else, shouting loudly and holding their goods high up above their heads so we could see them through the bus windows. None of them got run over but I expected it constantly. A passing thought worried me: that my life could turn out this way, that at some unexpected moment some unpredictable event might occur to make me so poor that I would be forced by circumstance to try and earn my living selling wares to passing traffic. Constantly, when in Pakistan, I am reminded how much easier – and safer – our lives back home in Europe or North America can be.

As a mountain guide, my self-employed way of life does feel pretty fragile; there is no sick pay or affordable insurance cover so if I damage myself, or if clients do something unpredictable and I sustain an injury, I could be out of a job. On the other hand, here I was, squeezed in with my friends among all this gear and travelling to the start of a great adventure. I knew how lucky I was. I felt paradoxically excited and relaxed. Exhausted from the journey, I expected sleep to come but, watching the disorganised splendour of the Pakistani countryside, the hustle and bustle of towns and villages, I found myself captivated and happy to stay in the flow.

The rest of the team seemed equally lost in their thoughts. From my seat at the back of the bus I could see them all. Now that we were together, sharing a ride to the mountains, I felt content with how I'd put the team together. Seeing Rick on the bus, a couple of seats in front of me, explained a good part of my confidence: Rick wasn't really chosen, he was simply the person I could trust most to be with on such a big climb.

Although in the valley we aren't the closest of buddies, we have known each other for decades, cutting our teeth on hard winter climbs in Scotland and meeting in the Alps as young apprentices. We shared an incredible adventure on the south face of Pumori almost thirty years ago. Two days into that climb, we were hauling our rucksacks up steep ground late in the day when the tent, which was tied to the outside of Rick's sack, got caught on a rock and came free, disappearing like a torpedo into the abyss. After a cold bivouac, the weather wasn't promising. The sky was overcast and cloud was blasting across the face. Clinging to our ice tools, we were strafed by falling ice and spindrift, but it never occurred to us to turn back. We spent the next night in a tiny snow cave and two days later reached the summit as the weather improved and conditions on the face became easier.

Rick had endured an even longer first ascent on the south face of Ganesh II with Nick Kekus, a guide like me. That was a twelve-day epic of tough and often dangerous technical climbing on a peak that is, like Pumori, over 7,000 metres. Nick and Rick endured some desperate bivouacs and towards the end, the weather turned bad and they ran low on food and gas. It was, until Nanga Parbat, the longest Rick had spent on a single push on a mountain, and it gave him a lot of confidence in how far he could take things. He also had plenty of experience on 8,000-metre peaks; Rick had been part of an otherwise Russian team that made the first ascent of Dhaulagiri's north face in 1993.

There have been very few new routes on 8,000-metre peaks by British climbers since the deaths of Peter Boardman and Joe Tasker on Everest in 1982. Their loss, attempting an alpine-style first ascent of the mountain's north-east ridge, cast a long shadow. To our generation, coming hot on their heels, there was a realisation that pushing big new routes on big mountains in the best style could be very dangerous. In 1985, Rick and I were part of an expedition led by Mal Duff that attempted the same ridge. We understood perfectly well what would be involved on Nanga Parbat. We had spent a lifetime preparing for it.

In recent years, during the summer of 2009, Rick and I had

reached the summit of Nanga Parbat via the Kinshofer route on the Diamir side. This was first climbed in 1962, on one of the many expeditions to the mountain led by Karl Herrligkoffer. (It's known as the Kinshofer after one of the lead climbers, Toni Kinshofer. Herrligkoffer was an expedition organiser, not a climber. That could and did lead to tension.) Conditions had been very windy near the top, but our climb had been a happy experience. Even so, both on the way up and down, my eyes and mind were often on the Mazeno. I must admit that while it looked corniced and convoluted, and was without doubt a very long ridge indeed, I felt sure in my mind that if any team could climb it, Rick and I could. Indeed I was not alone in thinking this. At one point, when Rick and I had spent several nights at Camp 3 acclimatising, we came back to Base Camp for a rest and seriously considered abandoning our Diamir climb in favour of the Mazeno.

Fortunately, better sense prevailed; as we discussed it Rick and I realised we weren't ready. I knew we hadn't sussed out a sound plan that would give us a chance beyond the Mazeno Gap. Rick was happy to go and try; he would have gone on the Mazeno at any cost, knocking his head against any obstacle, but some of the world's best had reached the gap exhausted and had needed to fight hard to escape the ridge and get back down alive. After careful consideration we decided to continue with our climb of the Diamir. It turned out to be a grand summit and the knowledge gained was well worth the time it took; having first-hand knowledge of the descent would come in handy for any future attempts on the Mazeno. Quite by chance, my sister Eunice also thought that with our ascent I became the first Scotsman to climb Nanga Parbat.

Even though Rick and I have a high level of trust in each other, we often have what Rick once described as 'lively discussions'. Rick is tough – a hard, steely nut. In comparison, I am Mr Softy, too emotional and sensitive for my own good. Rick believes that if you hit a problem over the head often enough it eventually breaks. He uses phrases like 'our efforts were vindicated', as though climbing is a war against the elements. I have learned, sometimes through bitter experience, that pushing hard does not always work out well, in life as well as the mountains. I knew we had to come up with an alternative strategy. I wanted to get to know and understand every aspect of the mountain and work with it, to understand it and perhaps be lucky enough to co-exist with it long enough to reach the summit. Whether it would let you get down from the summit was a different matter, but that was a bridge we would only need to cross if we got to the top.

Rick and I had spent almost twenty years talking about the Mazeno, starting with that first attempt in the mid 1990s. That's when the obsession began. It was a problem we couldn't let go. It took many years for a plan of how we should climb the ridge to evolve. For a long time I argued we could do it on our own; Rick believed we should have a bigger team. He knew my cash flow was always tricky and I might have to pull out for financial reasons. Getting time off from his job in the oil industry took a lot of advance planning with his employer. If we went with a bigger team, then he'd have reserves if I pulled out.

I couldn't see that bringing more climbers added anything, especially if they weren't as experienced. Like a chain, the expedition would only be as strong as its weakest link. But, as the years passed, I began to see things differently. It became clear how physically and mentally exhausting reaching the summit from the Mazeno would be. Swenson and Chabot had arrived at the Mazeno Gap too depleted to continue. The fact that they had been able to reach the Mazeno Gap at all was inspiring enough, but there seemed little point in repeating the exercise. I did not want to be involved in yet another attempt that climbed the ridge but failed to reach the summit.

So I found myself conflicted about how to proceed. I knew I wanted to go back with Rick. But I also knew there was little prospect that we would have the energy to climb the ridge, carrying all the necessary gear and food, breaking trail for all those kilometres, over all those summits over 7,000 metres, and then continue up to the summit of Nanga Parbat at over 8,000 metres. Given the scale of the challenge and the cost of the enterprise, I asked myself again and again if we weren't crazy just to contemplate such an adventure. It began to make sense to take more people.

Having decided to enlarge the team, we looked around for climbers to join it. This is always a lot harder than people might imagine. There aren't so many people around who have the depth of experience, talent and ambition to take on a challenge like this. I spend a lot of time in the Alps among kindred spirits and great friends who are constantly climbing magnificent routes there and around the world. They are amazingly competent and ambitious mountain climbers. But when I asked them to come with me to the Mazeno Ridge, none of them seemed that interested. One young pal, a guide, showed some real interest but his mate and regular climbing partner wasn't so sure. His wife had just had a baby and the Mazeno was no place to think about your duties as a new father.

Rick also mentioned Andrew Lock, an Australian he had climbed with a lot. Andrew had also been with us in 1995 when we first tried the ridge with Doug Scott and so he knew the challenge of the Mazeno well. I'd run into Andrew since then, and discovered just how reliable he could be. I had been guiding a private client up Everest when I discovered someone had wandered off with my ice axe, which I'd stashed at Camp 3 on the Lhotse Face. Fortunately for me I met Andrew, on his way down from the South Col. I asked him if he would lend me his axe, and he didn't think twice about it. Only a true friend does something like that. So I was tempted to go along with Rick's suggestion, but I was still having doubts about the tactics we should be using on the mountain. I wondered again whether someone else, even another strong climber, could contribute enough, knowing they would simply add weight with the extra food and gas. Our dreams drifted along, half-formed and uncertain.

Then a friend and fellow mountain guide called Ewen Todd said he wanted to come. Ewen is a great guy, a wild card indeed. He and his older brother Willie, who is also a guide, grew up in the village of Braemar, a place almost as remote as my home village of Dalwhinnie. Ewen had climbed the north face of Les Droites above Chamonix at the age of sixteen. At that time, a fair few years ago, the Droites' north face was a testpiece and Ewen had climbed it with ease. Both of us work in the world of industrial rope access and I have known him for years. Even though we had never really climbed together, I just knew it would be great fun to be on the mountain with him.

Ewen's wife Carrie invited me to their house in Aviemore, where their fantastically energetic children were climbing over the furniture. I took with me a large framed print of a photograph that had hung on my wall at home for a number of years. Taken by Doug Scott and gifted to me by my former wife, it showed the Mazeno Ridge in all its complex splendour. Drinking tea at Ewen's house I explained the objective, tried my best to point out the main features and my simple plan for climbing it. I could see the immensity of the ridge quickly made an impression, and then the extra bit, the 8,000-metre summit at the end … Ewen already knew all about Nanga Parbat and its famous tales of death and destruction. We talked a great deal and I felt at home with them and left with a positive feeling. But a few days later Ewen called to say that he wouldn't be joining us.

We weren't having much luck, but, despite these setbacks, the idea of having a couple more strong climbers with us on the ridge had become a concrete plan. I thought of my good friend Lhakpa Rangdu, who I had met guiding in Nepal. I first hired Rangdu – and Zarok too – through my agent Chowang Sherpa who runs Arun Treks and Expedition in Kathmandu. He worked a lot for my old pal Mal Duff and it was through climbing with Mal that I began to get to know Chowang. When Mal died on Everest

I decided to use Chowang's company as my Nepali and Tibetan agent for my guiding company Team Ascent.

Rangdu has a warm smile and a long fringe and is a sensitive man, not at all macho. Most importantly, he has that sound balance of judgement you only find in the best. Lakpa Zarok has a longer face than Rangdu, and a toothy smile. He is happily married to a wonderful Sherpani, Pasang Limey Sherpa, who hails from Namche Bazaar, the Sherpa capital. 'Zarok' is actually a nickname, being a small village situated between Namche Bazaar and Khunde where there is an experimental yak-breeding farm. Between expeditions he spends much of his life with his wife looking after their trekking shop in Namche. Like many Sherpas, the hard and risky work on expeditions can bring in relatively high wages, allowing their children to attend private schools in Kathmandu while their parents spend a lot of time travelling back and forth between Namche Bazaar and the Nepalese capital.

Zarok and Rangdu have become good friends, working with me on several of my commercial Himalayan guided expeditions. We've pulled off some good ascents with our clients. Both men are very strong, but Lhakpa Rangdu's leadership and his understanding of Western psychology are very shrewd, acquired over many years working as a sirdar, or lead Sherpa. He climbs well and has travelled widely. Like many Sherpas, he started his career as a humble cook boy, working his way up to cook before eventually becoming a climbing Sherpa and then, thanks to his management skills, responsible for the running of expeditions. As he climbs technically very well he has been accepted to become an IFMGA mountain guide and as I write this he is diligently working towards becoming fully qualified.[3]

Rangdu has reached the top of Everest nine times, as well as the summits of other 8,000-metre peaks in Nepal, like Cho Oyu,

---

3 He subsequently became a qualified guide.

Kangchenjunga, Manaslu and Lhotse. Zarok had climbed Everest seven times, as well as Cho Oyu and Kangchenjunga. Even though Zarok and Rangdu are outstanding high-altitude workers, lugging clients' gear up and down the slopes of the normal route on Mount Everest, they also try to get work on more exciting adventures. In 2009, three years before our trip to Nanga Parbat, Rangdu and Zarok had worked for me guiding a client called Becky Bellworthy to the summit of Baruntse, where she became the youngest person to climb that peak. (She also climbed Everest in 2012, after recovering from a stroke she suffered there in 2011.) It was on that Baruntse trip that I really began to think that these two Sherpas were truly exceptional and that they would be great partners to have on a big new climb like the Mazeno. I showed them some photos I had on my laptop and asked them both to visit Ang Phurba – the same Ang Phurba who had accompanied Doug Scott on his first exploration attempt on the Mazeno back in 1992. He had also been an important member of Chris Bonington's Sherpa team on the south-west face of Everest in 1975.

I knew Ang Phurba would advise them well. On another expedition we had spent a lot of time together shooting the breeze, drinking tea at his family house in Khunde and their other teahouse at Sanasa, a small hamlet on the main Everest Base Camp trekking route. Although Rangdu lived mainly in Kathmandu, he spent a lot of his time in the Khunde area, where Zarok lived in the adjacent village. I told them both to get Ang Phurba to explain in their own language about Pakistan and how long and difficult the climb would be. I asked them to think hard about the Mazeno as it was such a serious undertaking. I wanted the two Lhakpas to fully understand as much as they could about the climb and what it involved. Given the problems of finding the right people, it was still more or less a pipe dream in my own head – although I knew that, eventually, I would be going back to attempt the Mazeno again.

I suppose to other climbers peering in at our expedition it was a strange decision. Why would I want Sherpas when there are so many Western climbers? Perhaps some people don't understand that some Sherpas are more than capable of doing a climb like this. They assume Sherpas are all about carrying bags for other people. That view of the Sherpas is very outdated now, with so many training to become qualified IFMGA guides. On commercial expeditions Zarok and Rangdu routinely work out in front fixing ropes or supporting other lead Sherpas. The number of Western climbers strong enough to do this sort of work, fixing rope and breaking trail while carrying heavy loads, is fairly small. As we get older and our strength diminishes, we have learned to trust the really good Sherpas to get on with it and they do an exemplary job by themselves.

Some Western clients don't give sufficient credit to climbing Sherpas. They sometimes give the impression on their websites or in expedition reports that it is they themselves who lead the trip. Plenty of well-known Western leaders and clients benefit from the Sherpas' hard work but fail to mention it in their dispatches back home. But as mountain guides taking clients to the higher peaks most years, our and many others' expeditions would have little success at all if it were not for the Sherpas. They are truly exceptional. When I was younger, and once I was acclimatised, I could just about keep up with the Sherpas. They would sometimes call me Sherpa Sandy, which I took as a huge compliment. But even back then I was glad to get a heavy pack off my back and grab a quick rest, or to take it easy by following in the footsteps of a Sherpa when the chance arose.

The Sherpas do this too, taking care of each other, leading for a while and then letting someone else take over. They have good systems of leadership and teamwork – much of it unspoken. The younger ones defer to the experience and wisdom of older Sherpas. I feel so lucky to have witnessed this system of apprenticeship and sense of brotherhood. As I have grown older I find it harder and harder to be out in front. When climbing in pure alpine style it's necessary, but progress can be achingly slow when the snow is unconsolidated and you have to break trail. Friends like Russell Brice, an amazing climber in his own right and one of the best Western operators on Everest, say the same. We can keep up for a bit, but doing it day after day like the Sherpas is no longer possible.

Rangdu was delighted when I invited him to Nanga Parbat and Zarok also seemed excited and pleased. When Cathy committed to the expedition, helping us to secure the necessary funding, we had the resources to pay the Sherpas' expenses. I also sent an email to Chowang at Arun Treks seeking a third Sherpa. He recommended Nuru, and I was really pleased with the suggestion. Although I hadn't climbed with him we had seen each other on the same big hills. Lhakpa Nuru, with his cool glasses and spiky hair, had also summited Everest nine times and his uncle is Ang Phurba, who offered such good advice to Rangdu and Zarok.

It should be clear now that finding the right Western climbers hadn't been that easy. The thought of carrying the weight of supplies required, for eight or ten days and up and over eight 7,000-metre peaks, just to get part way along a ridge, was a big disincentive. They knew the chances of success were incredibly thin. So, with all the usual human complications, the newly born babies, the happy marriages and so on, committing to such a vast enterprise was daunting. Me, I was happily divorced, my daughters were adults and while work was fine, there wasn't much to stop me. I had the time and the inclination. I also knew I had enough control over my own emotions to make the right decisions. The thought of actually losing my life on this route never even entered my head.

If Rick and I can help support the Sherpas, I thought to myself, sitting in the bus, and we all get through to the Mazeno Gap, then surely Rangdu and Zarok will still have the energy to go on to the top. Cathy was just in front of me, her long, freshly washed hair catching the sunlight. I knew she'd be strong on the hill and having a sound female influence in the team could only be good. I was so glad she was here. Years before we had climbed together on Lhotse West above the Western Cwm and since then we have run into each other in interesting cafes from South Africa to remotest Tibet. Cathy's contribution to finding sponsors had made this expedition possible. She would be running the expedition's website and online social networking, and had bought all sorts of battery-hungry communications equipment to meet these needs.

In planning the expedition, she had said a few times there was no way that she would even get to the summit pyramid and would probably have to turn back. That was the reason I had decided to invite a third Sherpa, to take her down safely. I explained to her that Rick and I would push hard and not go down until we got to the Mazeno Gap, on the basis it was safe to do so. She understood we would want to make the most of our attempt and not waste the effort and resources we'd put into getting us up there. The level of commitment was incredibly high, and we couldn't lose sight of the main objective just because one of us got exhausted or disen-chanted with the idea. If Cathy, or any one of us, had to turn back then we would have to go down with a Sherpa. That was a given.

Even so, I had no doubt at all that Cathy would get high on the ridge. I liked her energy and I knew her strength, her determination and her intelligence. Over the years Cathy has been caught up in a lot of controversy, little of it her fault. She had climbed Everest in 1996 during that famous, tragic season captured in Jon Krakauer's book *Into Thin Air*. She had been part of that first South African Everest expedition, which had the backing of Nelson Mandela. Cathy was still feeling her way as a climber back then, but the team had included some of South Africa's best-known climbers and mountaineers. They had fallen out with the leader, Ian Woodall, and taken their toys home, assuming that the inexperienced Cathy would soon give up. She didn't, and both she and Ian reached the summit, although a third team-member who also reached the top, the British photographer Bruce Herrod, died while descending. Cathy and Ian later climbed Everest from the north, Cathy becoming the first woman to summit the peak from both sides. She and Woodall had been married but were now separated; Cathy I think was still feeling bruised by their separation and Nanga Parbat would be a welcome distraction. In all the years I'd known her, Cathy had shown commitment in the mountains and incredible determination.

Of course we would miss anyone who had to go down, but as a high-altitude climber you have to be a chess player. Years of working in extreme environments, whether in remote mountain areas or on the North Sea, have taught me something: to keep plans very simple and avoid building in complexity – that way I can react quickly to whatever happens. We were all equals on the Mazeno; the Sherpas were climbers in their own right. It was not their role only to carry and support us and they would certainly have the strength to keep going if Rick or I became exhausted on the ridge.

I didn't much care whoever got to the summit, only that some of us did. That was my goal. We would all look after one another and do everything possible to support the stronger climbers and then get down safely when the time came. Each of us would be climbing for the others, six people with one mind, with the primary aim of getting as many of us as possible to the Mazeno Gap so that maybe, just maybe, there would be enough supplies to give some of us the energy to continue to the summit.

02

MENTORS

Driving through the Pakistani countryside, I rested my head on the window and thought of all the people who, over the years, had got me here. Mal Duff had been there at the start of it all. He was part of the reason I was on this bus now. I remembered waiting for another ride, from London's Victoria station to Chamonix for one of Mal's legendary climbing courses. He had sent me joining instructions through the post, because that's how things were done in the 1970s. We were to make our own way to London and meet at an appointed hour under Victoria's huge departures board. Mal would gather up his latest recruits and we'd all drive off together – only it didn't work out that way.

As a nineteen-year-old lad, I was looking forward to my first season in the Alps. I'd learned the basics of rock climbing near my home in the Cairngorms. I had spent long evenings poring over books by famous climbers, from Albert Frederick Mummery and Edward Whymper to Gaston Rébuffat and Lionel Terray. My biggest inspiration, as a Scot, was the Edinburgh climber Dougal Haston who, in 1966, had climbed a new route on the north face of the Eiger after John Harlin had fallen to his death. Then, in 1975, Haston survived an unplanned bivvy above 8,000 metres on the south-west face of Everest with Doug Scott. I knew that both of them had climbed with a fellow called Chris Bonington, who seemed good at getting media attention and had written a book called *I Chose to Climb*, which was open and honest, inspiring and quite different to other mountaineering books of that time. Doug, who looked a bit like John Lennon, and Dougal were all over the news thanks to their success on

Everest. Their mountaineering achievements inspired a generation – my generation.

So I found myself walking across the concourse at Victoria where a number of other youths waited for Mal under the departures board. We introduced ourselves, sniffing round each other in the way that young men do, trying not to appear like we cared, but caring a great deal. They seemed far more streetwise than me. Some had sprouted immature beards and had grown up in the city. I felt very much the country bumpkin. This was my first adventure away from home. Even the train down to London had been a novel experience. The only other train I'd been on was the small puffer we had at Balmenach Distillery, where my father worked.

The engine was owned and maintained by the distillery and ran down to the main line at Cromdale where it would pick up wagons left in a siding. The little engine would hitch up the big wagons, loaded with tons of coal or barley, and pull them back up to the distillery, where they were unloaded by men with shovels. The barley was turned to malt, a vital ingredient for the final amber spirit; the coal powered it all. With my twin brother Gregor and younger sister Eunice, I'd hitch rides on the train to visit the local shop and play with other kids.

Balmenach is an excellent whisky, a 'single malt' that without doubt is one of the very best from Speyside. Not only was my dad a distiller, so was his father before him and almost all my uncles on that side of the family. My mother was from farming stock and we have many relations who own large parts of the Black Isle and drive those big green John Deere tractors that delay motorists driving along the A9.

When Greg and I were born, our parents were running the distillery at Dalwhinnie, in a wonderfully isolated spot in the Cairngorms often mentioned on the news as the coldest place in Britain. My dad had driven Mum to Raigmore Hospital in Inverness when we arrived on 8 September, with me emerging fifteen minutes ahead of my brother. We have been good buddies since birth and have an uncanny connection to each other. To this day, one of us can pick up the phone to call the other and be connected without the phone ringing at the other end of the line. We have even gone out to buy ourselves the same new car – the exact same model, same colour and everything – without even hinting to the other that we were buying a new vehicle.

Greg now lives in the Channel Islands. He doesn't climb but the bond we have gives me fantastic strength. He left school with ambitions to become a chartered accountant while I wanted to be a shepherd and whisky distiller. He now runs his own company advising large investment houses and multinational companies, and sits on the boards of huge financial institutions giving expensive and apparently sound advice. I am a shepherd in a way, shepherding people in the mountains, rather than sheep. We each have two daughters and all are the best of friends.

So there I was, a naive Highland laddie, standing in Victoria station daring to speak to these cosmopolitan youths apparently accustomed to crowds and swearing broadly, something I'd not heard at home. British Rail staff, many of them Afro-Caribbean, moved around us, the first black people I'd seen who weren't on television. My Karrimor 'Haston Alpiniste' rucksack showed the wear and tear from years of Munro-bagging and other adventures in the Scottish Highlands, but otherwise I felt I was the novice of the party.

Hours later an older man with a proper beard approached us. He was quite skinny and had a fine, clear Edinburgh accent – Mal Duff. As he talked his arms waved. Our vehicle, supposed to transport us to Chamonix, had broken down. There were apologies galore. We were to board a train, pay for it ourselves, go to Dover, catch a ferry and then continue to Paris, where we would transfer by Metro to another station on the other side of Paris and catch another train to Saint-Gervais and so eventually on to Chamonix. He had no idea what trains to catch, which platforms they left from or a single clue about times. He winged it all the way, something I quickly learned was typical of Mal.

It was a mad but exciting rush between platforms, all of us running after him like chicks, bent double under our huge rucksacks. I was totally exhausted, having not slept since leaving Scotland, and I kept falling asleep, sitting on train floors since the seats always seemed to be occupied. Eventually, starving and bedraggled, we all tumbled out on to the platform in Chamonix to be told that it was only a mile or so to walk – in blazing sunshine – to the campsite.

This, it turned out, was on the wonderfully infamous Snell's Field on the outskirts of Chamonix. The place is a legend in Alpine-climbing tales, a wild camping area in more ways than one and still home to a famous boulder called the Pierre d'Orthaz. (We all thought it was named after some guy called Pierre, maybe the guy who owned the field.) Mal had a team of illustrious British climbers working for him, none of whom were qualified guides, at least not then. There were tents pitched haphazardly and a kitchen area with gas stoves, pans and a water butt. We were given a quick introduction to the camping area, our tents and sleeping places, and were handed mugs of hot tea with a sachet of powdered milk.

I hid my passport in my Blacks sleeping bag, something every British kid had at the time, and we walked into Chamonix for our first beer in the famous Bar Le National, a longstanding bastion of British climbing. By the bar sat the owner, a well-rounded man called Maurice Simond who seemed almost always half asleep. He had two wonderful daughters, Sylvie and Christine, who were both very welcoming. None of us could afford to buy more than one drink there and we soon learned to go to the supermarket and buy cheap bottles of beer before meeting up at the bar, where we would buy one beer from Maurice, drink it and then top up our glasses under the table. Maurice knew what we were up to but let it go, a kind man and welcoming to all British climbers. When he passed away many years later I wrote to the British Mountain-eering Council suggesting we do something on behalf of British climbers to mark his passing. A little brass plaque was fixed to the wall of the Bar Le National recalling his hospitality 'with thanks from all British alpinists'.

For a young man from the Highlands, Chamonix was an eye-opening experience. The girls were beautiful, always in their summer dresses, their legs tanned and long, and speaking English with French accents. Surrounding Chamonix, the mountains and rock faces were incredible; one could not look at them and not be inspired to climb. It was an amazing town back then, overflowing with free spirits. Everyone seemed to climb or live to be in the mountains; everyone I met seemed in some way unconventional. Real jobs, proper mundane work, was something to be put off until later. Years later. Most people had good enough climbing equipment and clothing, some even had good off-piste ski-mountaineering skis and climbed in the Himalaya, but otherwise we all avoided spending money on unnecessary stuff. Hitch-hiking was how we travelled, or by taking possession of someone's old banger of a car. Living on a shoestring was the norm.

Our 'guides' took us to the Bossons Glacier, in those days much closer to the road, and after a short walk through the pine-scented forest we arrived at the ice. (These days, with climate change and glacial retreat, it's no longer considered a safe training venue.) I had never really used ice climbing tools before. I had an axe with an adze and an axe with a hammer, and some long nail-like ice screws called 'warthogs' and some clever new tubular screws introduced by a man called Yvon Chouinard. I wrapped long neoprene straps across my boots and through the rings on my crampons in a very deliberate pattern. Strapping on crampons was considered an art form. Then, with the buckles done up, I stomped along the ice.

It's the most fantastic feeling, being able to tramp across slippery blue ice. Our guides top-roped us at first and apparently

I was good at it; I was soon climbing up and over ice walls with overhangs and even soloing about. I loved it – I felt I was born to do this. The next day we were up on the Aiguille du Midi and I was taking my first nervous steps down the razor-edge of the Arête du Midi. How anyone expected a sensible human to walk down it was quite beyond me. Now of course I laugh at myself and as a guide I can be up and down it dozens of times in a climbing season. I was roped to a guy called Paul, a good climber Mal had hired even though, like Mal's other 'guides', he had little formal training on how to look after me. But he did his best and gave me the confidence to proceed.

After that we climbed Mont Blanc du Tacul by the normal route and I relished every single moment. We came back to bivvy, illegally of course, at the cable car station on top of the Aiguille du Midi. It did occur to me that Mal's course was more than a little unconventional, led by a dreamer who inspired adventure. Then again, I could afford it. I would have never been able to afford a proper organised course with qualified Chamonix guides. After it was over I stayed on with one of the instructors and we climbed the Brenva Spur on Mont Blanc. I climbed Mont Blanc again that season with Dave Cuthbertson, one of the best climbers of his generation and a well-known guide.

We ended up traversing the mountain, and I remember walking back to Snell's Field with him, traversing the Géant icefall, climbing into and out of huge crevasses with Cubby keeping me safe on a tight rope. We continued down the miles of frozen ice of the Mer de Glace to Montenvers and down through the thick forest to the Pierre d'Orthaz and our scruffy tents. I had a brew, and fell asleep for fifteen hours straight. I woke delighted with myself and the whole world, confirming in my own mind that I was destined to be an alpinist. Handing the instructors a gift of Johnny Walker whisky I left Chamonix to return to my job at the Balmenach Distillery. It was the first time in my life I hadn't wanted to get back to work and life in Scotland.

Mal had disappeared into thin air by the end of the course. Nobody seemed to have much idea where he was but by now we didn't expect otherwise. Some of the others thought him a cowboy, but I liked him a lot, recognising he was a rough diamond, a dreamer – and so inspiring. He reminded me of my older brothers Max and William, who were always up to tricks but somehow always avoided getting into trouble. All the guides had been good fun, but Mal had something else. He was enterprising and a risk-taker. He read widely and seemed to retain every single word. Little did I know that he would influence my life again in the future, and that I would attempt to climb Everest with him.

In those days it wasn't really illegal to work as a mountain guide and not hold a proper qualification. No one seemed to care much back then. But the world was changing. A more formal approach to mountain activities was beginning to evolve. The UK was now in the Common Market, as the European Union was then known. Chamonix was becoming famous for qualified mountain guides; the names Croz, Charlet and Ravanel were among the famous local families who had swapped farming for the mountains. It was not unlike my own experience in the Highlands where people were born, worked and made their meagre livings in the hills. They understood the mountain moods and the many eccentricities of the mountain weather.

At that time I didn't like mountain guides much – although a few of us would go on to become IFMGA qualified guides in years to come. They seemed slow and pedantic, taking delight in elaborating needlessly on each step a good and prudent guide should take but instinctively knows anyway; the type of person that felt it necessary to explain what most people with an ounce of practical ability would know from birth. I suppose I should have been more understanding as many were city kids. I'd grown up a Highlander, running over the hills, chasing red deer as a feral five-year-old in the arctic conditions of the Dalwhinnie hills. They weren't so fortunate.

My twin brother and I worked on farms too, driving tractors and Land Rovers at an incredibly young age, shepherding sheep and rescuing beasts from big winter snows. We were fortunate to be so privileged. We learned naturally. It was a slow process climbing behind these guides, and at the time I thought so bloody English. I soon knew not to get stuck behind them and used to ask them rather bluntly to get out of my way. Now I can't believe how crass my egotistical behaviour must have seemed, but I couldn't understand how anyone could find ice climbing difficult. I had taken to it as a duckling takes to water. I cringe at the thought that I must have spoken harshly to some of these good and highly experienced guides.

Back home that autumn, my life in the world of whisky distilling went on, although I climbed more and more. Yvon Chouinard wrote *Climbing Ice*, a book with lots of technical information about the art of ice climbing, interspersed with tales of road trips through America in cars with white-walled tyres, climbing in Patagonia and beyond. It inspired me. I started winter climbing on Ben Nevis, and my first winter climb was *Vanishing Gully*, which, in those days of ice tools with straight picks, was considered one of the harder and more technical climbs around.

When we got down to Fort William that evening, everyone was very impressed. Alex MacIntyre was in the pub that night, the only time I ever met him, and he came over to congratulate us. He was one of those people that you know is special and strong as soon as you meet them. He had been doing some amazing climbs with Nick Colton and John Porter. Years later, after Alex died on the south face of Annapurna, I climbed with Voytek Kurtyka, who had known Alex well and climbed with him in the Himalaya. Voy often spoke of Alex, telling me how he'd been a poor rock climber but was great on ice. It's how I am myself. Many climbing partnerships are like this, relying on each other's strengths for the overall good of the team.

I climbed *Vanishing* with a pal introduced to me by Mal Duff called Robert Bruce, a direct descendant of *the* Robert the Bruce, whose family owned Glen Tanar Estate in Deeside. We teamed up with a young, long-haired American called Rob Milne who worked at Edinburgh University developing a system that allowed you to talk to computers. He was clearly an exceedingly intelligent and bright kid, and had established quite a reputation for bold leads on ice climbs. He showed us how to hang off ice screws, which was considered quite radical and even stupid by us Scottish climbers back then. He also climbed with Hummingbird picks on his Lowe ice tools. These were tubular and worked well on thick ice but often became bashed at the ends by the time he had climbed a typical Scottish route of rotten or thin ice.

I climbed with one Chouinard Zero hammer, which had a wooden shaft and a curved pick with teeth along its whole length. It was my pride and joy. In my other hand I used a Chouinard-Frost ice axe with just five little teeth at the end of the pick; it was pretty rubbish but if used well would let you climb very steep ice. Strapped to my feet I had Salewa crampons with stubby angled front points. To climb steep ice, I needed to really hang out on my crampons to allow the front points to penetrate the ice.

The technique and body positions I had to adopt helped me become a technically very competent ice climber. Once Hamish MacInnes brought out his dropped-pick Terrordactyl axes lots of us began to climb very technical steep ice and then moved on to the steep and technical mixed climbing on the buttresses and rock faces. With crampons on I was convinced I could climb almost anything. Simond, the Chamonix manufacturer, then brought out an ice tool named the Chacal. This was the first ice tool with an 'inverted banana' type blade, inspired by MacInnes's Terrordactyl but more finely machined with very sharp picks, well-designed teeth and a good shaft that one could grip with ease. It made ice climbing really quite easy.

I loved and lived for Scottish winters and while I spent my summers returning to Chamonix, I could hardly contain my excitement as I waited for the snow to fall back home. A river flowed past the distillery through a gorge and I would train on its steep and often unstable banks. There were also some old warehouse walls and a disused industrial chimney stack. I would climb these in crampons and ice axes, torquing the picks of my ice tools between the bricks and resting them on tiny holes or ledges in the concrete or between the brickwork. This type of climbing is now known as dry tooling, although in Scotland we still often call it mixed climbing. To me, mixed climbing is the best sport of all, where one climbs on thin ice, exposed rock and a mixture of both. The Cairngorms were good for this, from Lochnagar to Ben Macdui, since the granite there has lots of cracks that one could clear of ice and snow and place semi-reliable protection. It was much harder to find useful cracks on Ben Nevis.

My life in those days had a quiet simplicity. Having perfected our technique with traditional gear, the advances in ice tools and protection gave us the confidence to try harder climbs. With these modern ice tools, in the late 1980s my good friend Andy Nisbet and I climbed some of the first grade-VIII winter climbs. Some of them are still unrepeated today. Our ascents of *Grey Slab* on Coire Sputan Dearg, and *Black Mamba* and the *Rat Trap* on Creag an Dubh Loch caused quite a stir in the winter climbing community when we reported them. *Rat Trap* took seventeen hours and we had all sorts of fun and games with a broken pick and hypothermia.

What young climbers do now is simply incredible and the current generation amazes and inspires me. Mountains are still mountains though; understanding the weather and developing other skills like navigation and good practical mountaineering knowledge are still important parts of the game we play. Accidents occur and these days it's often experienced climbers who are involved. Some people say that this is due to young climbers developing skills at indoor climbing walls where objective hazards have been removed, and risk suppressed. Some say that climbers these days haven't had a proper apprenticeship in the unpredictable outdoors. This notion may have some truth in it, but it's much too simplistic an answer. I see lots of young climbers who are skilled and experienced.

It takes years and years to develop the necessary skills for mountaineering, and more years to develop the confidence to listen and canvass other people's views and opinions and then to dismiss the silly parts and take on board the useful stuff. It's hard for us not to be influenced by others, to know our own limitations and have the confidence to turn back in pressing weather. As in most things, if you think you are a master, you're kidding yourself. There is always more to learn.

When I was young, I benefited hugely from having some great mentors. One of them was Doug Scott, who features a lot in my story. I can hardly remember how I got to know him, but his son Mike often dossed in a plastic palace in Snell's Field and we hung out a lot. Chamonix is also where I got to know Mark Miller. Mark was totally sound and wholly inspiring. I rented a small and very basic *mazot*, or chalet, in a quiet but quite central location in Chamonix with a lot of grass and woodland behind. I remember barbecues out back, wrapped in blankets with our girlfriends, staring at the fire's glowing embers under a star-washed sky. We'd talk about everything, especially the long Alpine routes we hoped to climb. It was a fine mellow time.

By this time I was working on exploration oil rigs in the North Sea, and I always returned to Chamonix for breaks. I was earning amazingly good money for the time and had an old Mini that we charged around in. We partied hard. Coming back from the rigs, I'd meet my girlfriend and with Mark we'd go out around town, trying to see how many days we could keep going before going home to curl up in my *mazot*. Chamonix had a few establishments that allowed you to get a drink twenty-four hours a day as long as you bought expensive cocktails. Our record was four days straight. Then we'd all crash, eventually resurfacing to try a big Alpine route.

Alpine winter climbing was really serious in those days. Clothing was inadequate compared to now; it's easy to forget how important breathable fabrics and other developments were in allowing mountaineers to push the limits in hostile conditions. Weather forecasts were not as good then as they are today – there were no mobile phones, let alone the internet. Even good route descriptions were often non-existent. The Alpine Climbing Group newsletter was the main source of new route information, along with, of course, the Sheffield-based *Mountain* magazine.

Mark and I hung out a lot and I had enough money to buy him the occasional cable car ticket. Between our wild parties, we climbed constantly. One of the more famous things we did was the north face of Mont Gruetta, which had never had a British ascent, although Doug Scott and Roger Baxter-Jones had tried it. We survived despite consuming many little tabs of a cardboard-like substance with little mallard ducks printed on one side. I had no idea what the card was impregnated with but it turned out to be LSD. Man, that made us laugh. The route took way longer than it needed as we broke every rule in the book. We seemed to lose a day or two in the hut under the influence.

Our bivvy food on that climb was a tube of condensed milk, some packets of potato powder and dried bananas. Our last bivvy was in a wild storm which would have frozen most people to death. Mark and I just grinned through it all, frozen solid in our neoprene jackets. I seem to remember having a Gore-Tex jacket, but it was so expensive that I protected it under the neoprene layer so as not to tear it on the rough rock. The Gruetta taught me a lot and having a first British ascent was something we valued. Roger Baxter-Jones and other Chamonix guides and climbers knew what we had done and began to treat both Mark and me as serious people whose views and opinions were worth hearing. That all felt good and was an acknowledgement that we were indeed growing up.

I went away to work on the rig in the North Sea and was pissed off to read a report by Lindsay Griffin that 'Mark Millar' had done the climb with some unknown Scot. No wonder we had a chip on our shoulders. It did seem that no matter how well we climbed, Sheffield magazine editors never had anything positive to say about us, whereas if a climber was English you were the best thing since sliced bread. I didn't want to be famous, but I did want to be acknowledged by my peers.

I actually spent quite a lot of time in Sheffield. I was holed up for a while with Mark in a rented flat on St Ronan's Road with some of the legendary 'Alpine binmen' – like Sean Smith and Murray Laxton. Mark and I were climbing hard, were now both broke and had one pair of rock shoes between us. He was technically a much better rock climber than me; even now I still feel a level of self-doubt about my rock climbing ability. But we got on so well that we had the necessary synergy to get up stuff, swapping leads and sharing the rock shoes and the chalk bag. Mark had put up a small testpiece called *Sex Dwarves* and we played on that lots. In my scatterbrained way I got the name wrong. I remembered it as 'Pink Dwarf', which is actually a kind of Japanese maple, and I put up several 'Pink Dwarfs' after that, one on a remote crag in the Lairig Ghru and another in Northern Ireland.

If Mark was stronger on rock, the roles were reversed on ice. He would smash his way up ice pitches, breaking ice tools and bending his crampons. In those days ice axes often broke, but I only ever broke one and that was on the blackest, hardest winter ice in the Alps. When Mark and I did a very early ascent of the *Supercouloir* on Mont Blanc du Tacul the ice was incredibly hard – 'harder than a Millwall supporter' was how Mark described it. When I tried to hammer in a warthog it bent like a carpenter's nail against metal. The warthog jumped out of my gloved hand and bounced down the climb, narrowly missing Mark. He'd already dropped most of the rack when he opened his rucksack after crossing the bergschrund. We climbed it anyway, without placing much protection, because we were climbing so well in those days and the idea of actually falling off never occurred to us.

Most young climbers go through this stage of feeling invincible.

Money was tight but we had a great time. Magic mushrooms, readily acquired in the Peak District if you knew where to look, were part of our staple diet, with pasta and tomato sauce and sometimes an onion. I remember being in Hathersage one sunny spring day, being so affected by whatever concoction of drugs Mark had given me that I could actually see the veins in the leaves of a sycamore pulsating with the liquids they sucked up from the earth. That night we dossed out in the hills above Sheffield and awoke to a vision of golden pools floating over the city's industrial landscape. We stood there, in a trance, shouting: 'Pools of gold, pools of gold!' We realised later it must have been the rising sun reflecting off the conical roofs of some big gas storage tanks near the motorway. That's about as romantic as Sheffield got.

Mark would get his girlfriend to paint his eyes and we would climb in whatever clothes we woke up next to in the morning. Black tights and tank-top T-shirts, often tie-dyed, was a favourite combination. God knows how we must have appeared and fortunately there are no pictures. Geoff Birtles was the editor at *High* magazine and seemed convinced Mark, myself and perhaps some of the others who dossed in St Ronan's Road were gay. We have no idea why he started such a rumour, but we just laughed about it. Such tight climbing attire was actually very practical, being warm but light, and became the fashion at that time. Still, it makes me cringe a little, thinking of us wearing old woolly jumpers from charity shops and thick, girls' tights.

Living in Sheffield, I came across some of the big stars of British alpinism at the time. Alan Rouse, who died in 1986 on K2 after making the first British ascent, was an influence on our lives. Al, Roger Baxter-Jones and Rab Carrington had done an impressive new route on Jannu in the Himalaya which massively impressed us. I had known Roger for many years through a mutual friend; he would stay at my rented house – in reality two big caravans welded together at Aultcharn in a remote glen by Grantown-on-Spey. Roger was doing his British Mountain Guides winter test and we did some routes on the Shelter Stone as practice.

At first, I wasn't sure about Al; I thought him a bit of an ego-head. But without the cash to drink in pubs, we'd often end up at Al's house smoking dope through a World War Two gas mask and having a wild time. Rab, a Scotsman who had the misfortune of being born in England, was also really helpful to me. He and his wife Sue, one of the kindest women I ever met, were often in The Moon Inn in Stoney Middleton and were working hard at a new small business making down sleeping bags. Paul Nunn, a central figure in British mountaineering at that time, also became a mentor, perhaps because I'd climbed with his old mate Richard McHardy and by that time a little with Doug Scott.

Sooner or later the wild times had to end. I had to call a stop to it all. The drugs thing was too much for me. Having had a strict upbringing, I had such a guilt-trip about it all and didn't like the flashbacks that were becoming more common. Things came to a head on a particularly bad trip: it was grey and wet and we couldn't climb, even on the gritstone walls around the city. I must have been in a really bad way as Mark and the others decided the best thing for my own safety was to lock me in a room with just a bed in it at the top of the house.

I woke up in the small hours with no idea where I was. I had just one thought: I have to end this and get away from here. So I tied my climbing rope, my most prized possession, to the bed post and abseiled out of the window, leaving it behind. Then I hitched north and caught a train to the village of Kiltarlity where I had a room at my parents' house. I arrived in the wee small hours after my parents had locked the doors. Dad found me in my sleeping bag by the doorstep with the milk bottles when he came out in the morning.

Mark and I stayed close but we didn't climb together much after that. Although the colours in my brain were wonderful, my body knew I had to leave that stuff behind. These days my sensible and wonderful daughters Hannah and Cara look at me in dismay when I tell them about those few months in my past life. I was lucky to get out of it without any lasting consequences. Mark went on to fall in love with a wonderful woman and set up an adventure climbing company called OTT with one of our friends, Andy Broom. Flying to Kathmandu in 1992 to lead one of their adventures, Mark's Pakistan International Airlines flight smashed into a mountain on final approach. There were no survivors. Several other good British climbers were on the aircraft, including instructors and guides from Plas y Brenin, the national mountaineering centre in Snowdonia. There is a memorial plaque to them there and I think of these guys often. But there is no mention on the plaque of my closest ever friend Mark Miller, who could have become one of Britain's most amazing alpinists.

After abseiling out of Mark's window I didn't go back to Sheffield until I had to get my rock climbing standard up when I started training for my guide's exam. In my early youth I seemed to have trouble with places like Plas y Brenin and its Scottish equivalent, Glenmore Lodge. I have no idea why, but I suspect it was down to being young and not liking any notion of boundaries or rules or institutions. All the people I met at such places were always incredibly kind to me and I know full well that their work is invaluable. Still as Groucho Marx said, marriage is an institution and who wants to live in an institution?

Fred Harper was the principal at Glenmore Lodge and was not only a competent mountaineer and guide but a true gentleman. Over the years he became a good friend who supported me as I qualified as a guide and when I was going through my divorce. I made some good friends at Glenmore Lodge, well-known climbers like Allen Fyffe, Bob Barton and Martin Burrows-Smith. I also got to know some great guys at Plas y Brenin, especially Rob Collister, Dave Walsh and Nigel Shepherd, but I never felt comfortable there, as though I was being judged for living on my wits. I know that assumption was wrong and I have a great regard for these institutions nowadays. Climbing would be a lot more dangerous without them.

As I grow older I realise how precious the world is and how wonderfully fortunate we are to still be alive. Mal Duff and Mark Miller are both gone, so are Al Rouse, Roger Baxter-Jones, Alex MacIntyre, Rob Milne and Paul Nunn. Apart from Mark, they all died in the mountains. I often reflect on how much Mark has missed in life. I think of him most days. I have no idea what our lives would be like if Mark was here now. I guess it would be like the TV programme *Last of the Summer Wine*, except on a crag, with all those ageing faces that still remain. I am no longer strong or daft enough to think I am invincible but I still get a huge feeling of self-confidence when I strap on my crampons and have good ice tools in my hands.

When I set off on a huge adventure like Nanga Parbat, all those climbers who helped me along the way come with me.

03

THE ROAD TO NANGA PARBAT

The drive along the Karakoram Highway is an astonishing journey through one of the most inspiring and wild regions of the world. Its construction transformed access to Pakistan's mountains. When Mummery and his friends travelled to Nanga Parbat in 1895, they were two weeks at sea to Bombay on the P&O steamship *Caledonia* and then spent two days travelling by train to Rawalpindi, the largest military cantonment in what was then British India and a hub of colonial rule in the north-western sub-continent.

From Rawalpindi they travelled first to Murree, where Henry Whymper, brother of the Matterhorn climber Edward Whymper, established a brewery in the 1860s. But then, instead of heading north as we did, they turned east into the Vale of Kashmir. The Ghurka officer Charles Granville Bruce, who later led the first Everest expeditions, also travelled east from his posting in Abbottabad to meet Mummery at Baramulla, north of Srinagar, and help him organise ponies and porters to carry their equipment. From Baramulla they travelled by punt up the Jhelum river to Wular Lake, thick with water lilies, marvelling at the beauty of Kashmir, before reaching Bandipur and the road to the mountains. They approached Nanga Parbat over the Kamri Pass, from where they got their first sight of the mountain, still forty miles away. It rose, Collie wrote, 'in dazzling whiteness far above all the intervening range. There is nothing in the Alps that can at all compare with it in grandeur, and although often one is unable to tell whether a mountain is really big, or only appears so, this was not the case with Nanga Parbat as seen from the Kamri.

It was huge, immense; and instinctively we took off our hats in order to show that we approached in a proper spirit.'

The road ahead proved hard for Mummery and his team; at one stage they had to build a bridge to get their mules across a river. But finally they reached Tarshing, a prosperous trading village under Nanga Parbat's immense Rupal Face on the south side of the mountain. We were also headed for Tarshing, but by a different route.

The Karakoram Highway, the 'KKH', begun in 1959 and still under construction in the 1970s, starts in Abbottabad and meets the Indus at Thakot seventy miles to the north. The road's construction from here to the Chinese border was mythically difficult. The death toll among workers has been estimated on the Pakistani side at around eight hundred – one person for every kilometre of road between Abbottabad and the Khunjerab Pass into China. Two hundred Chinese died on the other side of the border as the highway continued to Kashgar, on the ancient Silk Road.

Three of the world's greatest mountain ranges, the Karakoram, the Himalaya and the Hindu Kush, meet at Gilgit, a major staging-post on the drive north, so it's hardly surprising that this area sees frequent earthquakes. In 2005, an earthquake that measured 7.6 on the Richter Scale struck north-western Kashmir near the city of Muzaffarabad. Official estimates suggest 75,000 Pakistanis died, although international aid agencies put the death toll at more than 100,000. Thousands more were forced to abandon destroyed farms and villages and take shelter in refugee camps, having lost everything.

From Thakot, we followed the churning brown waters of the Indus, reaching Komila after forty miles, joined to the village of Dasu on the far bank by the KKH bridge. Here the road plunged into the Indus gorge proper for the eighty-mile drive to Chilas. The landscape was desolate, barren, rocky wastes punctuated by occasional terraces of green where irrigation had brought the mountains to life. The highway wound through a tangle of side ravines, often spanned by improbable bridges and threatened by huge piles of rubble; it seemed you would need only to touch them to send millions of tons of rock into the river.

Further north at Shishkat, much closer to the Chinese border, the KKH had been flooded by a lake that formed in January 2010 when a massive landslide blocked the valley. Goods and people were being ferried by boat to get past the blockage. When the dam created by the landslide gave way in June 2010, a wall of water up to sixteen metres high hurtled down the valley, destroying villages and killing thousands. Hundreds of Sikh soldiers at Attock were swept away as the flood caused damage hundreds of kilometres downstream. This sort of event is not new in the area – Collie described how he walked through the Indus gorge north of Nanga Parbat where an earthquake had blocked the river in 1841, creating a lake in six months that covered thirty-five square miles.

Every year the monsoon brings flooding and rockfalls and the KKH is under constant repair. The husks of crashed buses and trucks were a constant reminder of the road's formidable reputation for danger. Luckily for us, we were going only as far as Chilas, where there was an important police post. I'd travelled this way several times before, but on this journey we had a police escort all the way to Chilas. The security situation in Pakistan is often tense, but Pakistani Army operations against the Taliban in the nearby Swat valley were rumoured to have pushed Taliban fighters out of their bases to seek refuge beyond Swat's borders. Further north in Hunza, Western tourists could be sure of a warm welcome, but the situation in Chilas, with its more Wahhabi-influenced brand of Islam, was edgier.

A year after our expedition, ten foreign climbers and a local expedition worker were murdered at Nanga Parbat's Diamir Face Base Camp. Among the dead was Sona Sherpa, a good friend of Doug Scott's, who had worked on Doug's fundraising treks in

Nepal. He left behind a young family. A few weeks after the massacre, militants killed three members of the army and police team who were investigating the crime. The Taliban claimed responsibility, but the reasons for the attack – and the identities of the perpetrators – are still a matter of controversy. The murder not long before of Shia bus passengers in the Nanga Parbat region suggests sectarianism is rife in the district. Tourism has since suffered very badly, with local operators losing business. The road sign at Juglot featuring Nanga Parbat, the 'killer mountain', was covered up. The connotations were no longer worth people's attention.

The wild country around Nanga Parbat has always had a reputation for wild behaviour. The war correspondent Edward Knight came this way just before Mummery, researching his book *Where Three Empires Meet*. The heights of Nanga Parbat were, for Knight, a warning: 'That white horizon so near me was the limit of the British Empire, the slopes beyond descending into the unexplored valleys of the Indus where dwell the Shinaka tribesmen. Had I crossed the ridge with my followers, the first human beings we met would in all probability have cut our heads off.'

How the people keep smiling is hard to understand, but they do, like poor folks everywhere I suppose, making the best of what they have even though it is incredibly little. Wealthy people like us drive by in big four-wheel-drives and the poor people who watch still smile and joke around. Beyond the headlines, there are millions of friendly people in Pakistan. Edward Knight might have feared instant decapitation, but Norman Collie was more open-minded. The people of Chilas might have appeared, 'wild and unkempt, but throughout our expedition we found them to be friendly enough, and never experienced any difficulty with them.' He even admired their mountaineering skill.

Our bus driver drove and drove with only the briefest of stops at roadside restaurants. The boys serving smiled as they dished up rice, lentils and freshly baked paratha, but the toilets were filthy and so we balanced our hunger with the fear that we might get sick before the climb. The parathas were irresistibly tasty but with each bite I wondered if this was the mouthful that would leave me running for the loo for a day, three days or even a month and send me home before the expedition had even begun. Illness at this stage of an expedition is common and can play havoc with the best-laid plans. I've known some climbers take antibiotics prophylactically in anticipation of getting ill, but our group didn't entertain the idea. We knew any drugs could affect our performance. Our bodies would soon be at altitude and from long experience we knew that while acclimatising naturally may not be the fastest way to adapt, it is usually the best. If we took strong drugs now what would work when we got something we couldn't shake off?

Twelve hours after leaving Islamabad, at around 10 p.m., we spilled out of the bus in Chilas, a district town to the north of Nanga Parbat. Our trekking clothes, fresh on that morning, now stuck to our dusty bodies. The Shangrila Midway House Hotel was a home from home for Rick and me, having stayed there on previous expeditions, and our host greeted us warmly. The Sherpas were fascinated by the hotel's immaculately carved fretwork, both similar and different to the sort of carving so commonly seen in Nepal. Delighted to be off the bus, we made a vague plan for the morning before shouldering our rucksacks and drifting up to our rooms. Our main cargo was left strapped to the roof of the bus. I stood under the shower in our room, watching rivulets of water wash the dust from my body before climbing into bed.

As I lay in bed waiting for sleep I thought about how easy our journey had been along the KKH. The road still featured big potholes and tight bends, but had improved dramatically over the years. There were now trees and shrubs colonising the thin dirt at the side of the road, stabilising slopes that had been blasted apart during construction. Landslides on this stretch had once been common, but not now. I thought of the plaque I spotted by the side of the road that said: 'Some time in the future when others will ply the KKH, little will they realise the amount of sweat, courage, dedication, endurance and human sacrifice that has gone into making this road, but as you drive along, tarry a while to say a short prayer for the silent brave men of the Pakistan army who gave their lives to realise a dream now known as the Karakoram Highway.'

In 2012 we travelled comfortably in an air-conditioned bus, but I recalled my first journey along this road almost thirty years before, aboard an old converted truck with clunky suspension and clouds of diesel smoke. With wearying regularity we'd come across landslides where bulldozers and gangs of men with shovels were working to clear rubble. It used to be a continuous twenty-hour journey to Chilas, with the real fear of meeting robbers through the hours of darkness. Now it takes about ten to twelve hours to the North-West Frontier, gateway to our mountain and a relatively easy drive.

On that first trip, in 1984, I'd been on my way to Muztagh Tower. With my pals Jon Tinker, Tony Brindle and Mal Duff, who had gone from being elusive unqualified mountain guide to firm friend, we made the third ascent of the mountain and the second ascent of the north-west ridge. That was almost thirty years ago now – a lifetime of climbing.[1] When we came home from Nanga Parbat in 2012, people often remarked on our ages, as though what we were doing was somehow more remarkable because we were past fifty. I didn't really understand it then, and I still don't. In my head I still feel as enthusiastic and excited as ever, and while I'm not as strong as I used to be in my twenties and thirties, I've gained in other ways and don't see any reason to stop climbing until my body says 'enough'. I don't think I'm unusual in this. Steve Swenson, who reached the Mazeno Gap with Doug Chabot in 2004, was in his late forties when he did it, and is still climbing

---

1 That expedition is recorded in Andrew Greig's book *Summit Fear* (Canongate, 2005).

hard in the Karakoram. The Spanish climber Carlos Soria Fontán didn't do his first eight-thousander until he was in his fifties, and is still going strong in his mid-seventies, climbing Kangchenjunga aged seventy-five. Climbing is part of who I am. I still love doing it, so why should I quit?

Still, the body has to be kept in shape, and that doesn't get any easier. For training, I cycled on my simple Dawes hybrid, squeezing in a session early in the morning or late evening around my local circuit, leaving my house in Newtonmore, below the crags of Creag Dhubh, passing by Balgowan and riding through to Laggan, past my friends the MacDonalds at Drumgask Farm and up the hill to Catlodge, alternating the route sometimes by going by the Slimons' farm at Breakachy, or taking the longer hill towards Dalwhinnie and back along the old A9 to my home. The wind and rain were, more often than not, relentless. But I loved the hills of home slipping by and watching the wildlife – mountain hares, red deer and the occasional fox, with buzzards hanging overhead. Wild flowers changed with the season, and I once saw baby stoats playing among them on the verge. My most favourite of all was the evening call of the curlew, bubbling up from the darkening moors. It kept me company.

Fitness has never been much of a problem for me, whereas altitude can be. I take ages to acclimatise, absolutely ages. Even in the Alps I usually have to go high for a few days before guiding clients, playing Scrabble with the *guardien* at the 3,600-metre Cosmiques hut to kill time and adapt. That had been my plan before leaving for Pakistan but events had conspired against me. It didn't worry me too much. I may take a while, but once I am acclimatised, I am among the strongest people I know. I feel at home, comfortable in my own body above 7,000 metres. Being able to move efficiently in such a hypoxic and extreme environment is a blessing because I simply love being up there. I am also blessed with good circulation, but when I get tired I seem to feel the cold acutely, even in the Alps and Scotland. Sleep is vital to my wellbeing. Oh, I thought to myself, lying awake in Chilas, how I love to sleep.

After Muztagh Tower, I'd gone to Everest again with Mal Duff, to attempt its north-east ridge, the unclimbed ridge where in 1982 British climbers Peter Boardman and Joe Tasker lost their lives as they tried to traverse the pinnacles. Rick and I tried that ridge twice, in 1984 and 1987. On the second attempt we asked Doug to be leader, knowing that he'd be able to bring in the necessary support. I remember leading with Rick in thigh-deep snow and Doug commenting that he thought we were incredibly strong to do what we were doing, breaking trail at such high altitude. I felt a little bit of pride at that, Doug having climbed the south-west face ten years before.

Doug is a special man, with special abilities, and he passed on so much knowledge to me, perhaps unwittingly. I remember being with him high in the Karakoram, all of us freezing and complaining about the cold except for Doug. He was complaining he had a wrinkle in his sock that was bothering him, so he took off his boot while we stood there in the snow, freezing cold, shivering and urging him to hurry up. His feet were so hot we could see steam rising up out of his boot. I laughed so much that day, but I couldn't get over how Doug kept himself so warm.

Trying that ridge on Everest in the mid 1980s had been an incredible long shot and the same was true with the Mazeno. I knew how long it would take and that reaching the summit was incredibly unlikely. I knew the American climbers who first traversed it to the Mazeno Gap were incredibly strong and no less experienced than we. Technically there was nothing that would stop me from climbing it. It was the high altitude and the freezing cold that scared me. I lay in my warm bed in the Shangrila, imagining the frost forming on my skin and hair, the freezing spindrift being driven by the wind through the zips of my clothing, insinuating itself like an unwelcome squatter against the back of my neck. The thought of having to bivvy high on the mountain in such unbearable cold had me drawing the blanket up to my chin. Surviving where life should not exist and climbing through such hostile places is truly rewarding, but deserves the utmost respect.

That's why when Ewen Todd and other possible partners called to say they wouldn't be coming, I felt paradoxically reassured. It helped me realise that Rick and I really were the best team for the job. All our previous attempts on impossible-looking objectives on 8,000-metre peaks pointed in that direction. Rick was breathing quietly, asleep in the next bed. There is someone, I reflected, who fights until the very end. He will try and try at the same problem, anticipating that it will give way eventually. That's who he is, I thought, but it's not who I am. We had spent years arguing about this route. There was no way I was going to try on the off chance that this time it might work out. We had to be able to reach the end of the ridge and still have something left.

'It's still impossible,' I told myself, lying there in the dark, and yet somewhere in my brain was this unquenchable spark of belief, a kind of trust in the future. I knew inside me that we had the skills and the belief; Rick and I could do it. I just had to come up with a plan. And so I lay there, dreaming of the ridge, thinking of the audacity of what we were proposing, until sleep finally took me.

We rose late next morning – 11 June – and by the time we made it downstairs the Sherpas were smiling and happy, having ploughed their way through a huge breakfast. There was no rush. We took photos of Chilas and then climbed aboard the bus for the next leg of the journey. After twenty-five miles driving east, we turned south off the Karakoram Highway into the Astore valley and after a few hours reached the capital of Astore District, a town called Eidgah. We were now on the east side of Nanga Parbat. Here we switched to jeeps for the last bumpy stretch to the roadhead at the lovely village of Tarshing, where we pulled up at the Nanga Parbat Hotel. This was less a hotel and more a simple lodge, but with a large lawn in front where you could sit in the evening and take in the fabulous panorama of snow-capped mountains.

We were here much earlier than I'd planned. Our original idea was to go first to the Diamir, or north-western, side of Nanga Parbat to acclimatise. I thought we could climb a way up the Kinshofer route, perhaps to Camp 2 at around 6,500 metres. I've learned over the years that this is about the optimum height to get one's body properly acclimatised before going up to try an eight-thousander. Wasting energy going higher seems pointless to me; in my earlier climbing days we sometimes took the time to climb much higher but then became tired and exhausted before the main attempt. But even before we arrived in Pakistan, our agent Ali warned us that the mountains were still buried in feet of snow after an unusually harsh winter. The summer thaw hadn't yet cleared the way on the Diamir side, so in the interests of saving time, energy and the logistical complexity of having camps first on the Diamir side of Nanga Parbat and then moving everything to the Rupal side, we decided to focus our attention exclusively on our route up to the Mazeno.

The last time I'd been to Tarshing was with Doug, Rick, Andrew Lock and Voytek Kurtyka in 1995, arriving on a new-fangled contraption called a mountain bike. Doug had managed to secure sponsorship from the bicycle manufacturer Raleigh, which is based in his home town of Nottingham. Part of the deal required us to cycle their new mountain bikes across the Deosai plains that lie between Astore and Skardu, now a national park. This high summer pasture, according to one anthropologist, was the location for Herodotus' gold-digging ants – and that's what we were, singing if not for our suppers then for the expedition's coffers. Raleigh sent along cycling journalist Steve Thomas, who unfortunately got the runs, but did what he could and maintained our bikes for us. It took three days to cross the Deosai. The first night we camped above the beautiful Satpara Lake at 3,800 metres. The following day we reached the high plateau, often having to push our bikes along the stony, twisting track, wading rivers and crossing rickety bridges. The plain is high and remote, offering good grazing to flocks of sheep and goats. Local herders, as hefted as their animals, seemed to merge into the landscape.[2] I recall the whistle of marmots and huge drifts of wild flowers.

Crossing a high pass, our camping place that night was just beyond the Kalapani river, sixty-eight kilometres from Skardu. It was hard going for those of us new to off-road cycling and it rained hard next day as we crossed the Chakor Pass and then made the scary descent into the Astore valley. We reached Tarshing late that evening, splattered in mud and wet through, the bikes on the back of jeeps for the last bit along the road. Steve was to leave us next day but the torrential rain had washed away bridges and he remained trapped for a while. It was all great fun, but it left us depleted and full of colds and illness.

Like us, Mummery, Collie and Hastings arrived to discover bridges washed away, but from the south, not the north. Arriving at the village of Chorit, they found themselves unable to cross to the north bank of the Astore. No matter. There was soon a crowd of men on either side more than happy to help build a new one, as Collie described: 'The bridge-building began; tons of stones and brushwood were built out into the raging glacier torrent; next pine trunks were neatly fixed on the cantilever system in these piers on both sides, and when the two edifices jutted far enough out into the stream, several thick pine trunks, about fifty feet long, were toppled across, and prevented from being washed down the stream by our Alpine ropes, which were tied to their smaller ends ... after three hours' hard work the bridge was finished.'

Tarshing was still a simple place, although not as simple as it had been in Mummery's day. He had taken twenty-seven days to reach the village from Britain; we had taken three. Within minutes of our arrival the area around our parked jeeps had drawn a horde

---

2 'Hefted' sheep instinctively stick to their own local area and thus do not need fences.

of porters – like bees to a new hive. They crowded round the jeeps, smiling and looking expectantly for our sirdar. It felt great to be among this crowd of mountain men. I drew the fresh mountain air into my lungs and rested my eyes on the verdant green of the irrigated fields. Then Samandar Khan stepped forward from the crowd and shook my hand, and then hugged me in a warm embrace. It was ace to see him again and a relief too to find that Samandar would be our local fixer. I had gotten to know Samandar when we were climbing the Kinshofer route from the Diamir side. At that time Samandar was acting liaison officer for a Korean expedition led by the country's star climber Go Mi-Sun, who fell to her death after summitting Nanga Parbat, her eleventh eight-thousander. On rest days between acclimatisation forays I spent lot of my time shooting the breeze with Samandar as we sat in boulders around Base Camp. He lives in Bunar village, Chilas, and is married with five children. A thoughtful and kind man, he would share tales of his experiences of working with climbing expeditions in Pakistan. I made a mental note to thank Muhammad Ali for hiring Samandar.

We had met Ali in 2009 almost by chance. Rick and I, still dreaming of the Mazeno, had decided to climb Nanga Parbat's regular route on the Diamir Face. The plan was to climb as high as we could and at the same time get an impression of the ridge over a long period of time as well as experience of a possible descent route. While organising the expedition from my home in Newtonmore's old converted police station, I got an email from an Austrian guide called Gerfried Göschl who suggested I consider joining his much larger expedition. Gerfried had a lot of experience on 8,000-metre peaks, and had climbed Everest without supplementary oxygen in 2005. He also led expeditions for the Austrian Alpine Club.

We talked it over on the phone and it became obvious that with economies of scale we could travel and climb the mountain much more cheaply and with less organisational input from me by joining his large expedition. A tremendous additional bonus was that we got to know Gerfried's agent, Muhammad Ali of Adventure Pakistan. Ali had started his company in 2009, having worked previously for the Pakistan Foreign Office. As we camped and climbed with Gerfried we got to know and like him and many of his climbing companions. I found him to be a very kind and friendly individual, an exceedingly good climber and expedition planner – a chess player in negotiations. His father Rainer had also been a successful climber, part of Hans Schell's team in 1976 that made an important first ascent on Nanga Parbat's Rupal side.

Like many younger climbers, Gerfried was always taking photographs of himself, eager to please his sponsors. For someone of my generation, it's all rather terrifying, but a necessary part of the game. Himalayan climbing is expensive and for a guide like me – or Gerfried – the loss of earnings while on expedition can cost us dearly. True, we're away on 'holiday' having a fantastic time, but commitments back home carry on regardless. We still have to pay the mortgage and get the boiler serviced. Trying to anticipate what could go wrong is part of the preparation for an expedition so that there's the minimum hassle for the loved ones we leave behind.

Over the years Rick and I have needed to manage our time carefully and one great advantage of Nanga Parbat was its short approach. Rick's employers usually understand, but there's a limit. Despite the pressures, we both have the ability to suss out the really important issues and let the rest go. I liken it to birds migrating on their vast journeys across continents and oceans. Even though they fly for days at a time, they have techniques that allow them to coast along not really using up much energy at all, even though it seems they flap their wings like crazy to maintain momentum.

It's more difficult to explain to family that you love them and yet want to go away for several weeks to climb a beautiful but, as they see it, potentially dangerous mountain. As a climber I never think I'm not going to come home again; I'm confident the risk of an accident will be minimised and all will be fine. For family members back home, waving goodbye at the airport, there's the unarticulated thought: 'I wonder if I will see him again?' And while I feel confident of coming home, the truth is that there are risks. It's emotionally tough. In 2012 Gerfried himself disappeared attempting the Karakoram giant Gasherbrum I in winter, just three years after we climbed together on Nanga Parbat, when he added a new variant to the Kinshofer route.

Samandar had made all the necessary arrangements for the approach to Base Camp beneath the Mazeno Ridge. He had brought along an excellent cook with two young assistants and hired some experienced porters to help with all our equipment and supplies. In this part of Pakistan most loads are carried on mules but we anticipated that once we were at higher altitudes we would run into deep snow and the mules would most probably not be able to plough through it. Mules are worth a lot of money and the risk of injury would persuade the mule-drivers to turn back. So to make sure our loads got to Base Camp, we would take a few hardy men along as well. They would carry little at the start, but would increase their loads once we reached the snowline.

As the porters loaded up their mules in the village, local children passed by on their way to school, girls and boys together in their best school clothes. This was one of those rare occasions when we saw females mingling with the village crowd, even though it was only the children. Their mothers were out of sight, presumably busy in their homes. It was a part of Pakistani culture that I found hard to understand. How could a culture place such restriction on women's freedom of movement? It was all a bit strange really, to see so many people milling around and all of them men. What impact must this have on young men reaching maturity? I looked at the strong mountain porters setting out on the trail to Base Camp. Did they simply not trust their women?

Or themselves? Or was it visitors like us they didn't trust?

The approach walk was wonderful. We left the village on a well-maintained path, dodging mule droppings, stepping across irrigation channels and ducking under coppiced trees until we were free of the village. The day was pleasantly warm and we were happy to amble along taking in the views. The noise and dust of the Karakoram Highway felt far away and the hassles of day-to-day life fell away. Soon we would be able to focus on our climb.

The green terraces of crops and grass disappeared abruptly as irrigation ended, replaced with the wild and desolate terrain of a glaciated valley. The trail now wound its way through awkward moraine until eventually we came to a patch of more stable ground used for pasture where we could camp for the night. Its name was Latabo, a tiny hamlet at around 3,500 metres directly below the Rupal flank of Nanga Parbat. The place was rudimentary, just enough to support a few local people herding their sheep and goats. Here for the first time we saw women passing by and doing tasks amongst the animals. Not for the first time I reflected that life in the mountains is usually more egalitarian. Hardship makes it so.

I took the three Lhakpas and Cathy for a walk to show them the general direction of the Schell route. This we had earmarked as a possible descent route from the ridge, although to descend that way we would of course have to get all the way along to the Mazeno Gap first. Back at the planning stage Cathy kept highlighting that she really thought she would not get that far, and certainly not to the summit. However, I had a strong belief in her and felt she could, and would. I was pleased when she decided to accompany us for the walk. Unfortunately the summits were shrouded in mist so I could only point out the lower section of the climb, and from that distance there wasn't that much to see anyway.

We only had a short distance to walk next day; without acclimatisation we could not really go much higher without risking altitude sickness. So after a few hours of walking along an impressive glacier junction we traversed up towards an interim campsite. After setting up the tents and drinking a cup of tea, Rick and I took a walk several hundred metres above camp, to a point where I felt my head pounding a little bit with altitude. That was enough. With my head still throbbing, I flinched a little when we got back to camp to see the mules fighting, their huge, yellow teeth biting at each other's necks. I was sure one would get hurt and their loud braying pulsed through my head. I was glad when the porters and muleteers gathered them together and tethered the mules some distance from our tents.

We awoke to fresh snow on the ground and, as we gained height, the old snow pack became deeper, the mules sinking into the snow until only the longest-legged animals could continue. The rest of the mules had to be released from their loads, which were picked up by our porters. It was hard work freeing the mules in the deep snow, unstrapping the loads and rearranging them so a man could carry them. The daylight soon slipped away. Finally we got all our baggage moving again and at last came to the dry-stone-walled shelters used as base camps for previous attempts on the ridge, at an altitude of 4,900 metres. It was 14 June.

The snow was unseasonably deep and we had to hack away at it to reach hard ground on which to pitch our tents. All of us set to work. The cook and his team put up a much bigger mess and cook tent and, with slushy snow from a nearby pool warming up in a big pan set over a roaring paraffin stove, we began to pay off the porters. They drank and had a snack before we shook hands and waved each other goodbye. By the close of the day most had gone, although Samandar kept a couple on the payroll to help run Base Camp and organise our stores. One of them would also act as a runner for us, coming up to camp regularly with a supply of fresh vegetables from Tarshing.

As the sun set we were all still hard at work, trying to clear away snow and ice so as to have a base for our main mess tent. This would be our dining and living room during the day, somewhere to store equipment, eat our meals, hold meetings and rest. The snow was deep here and, with all the mule and porter traffic, had become quite consolidated. Yet by nightfall we had a large enough area cleared. We brought our barrels and climbing equipment inside and arranged it all around the walls, leaving a space in the middle for our collapsible tables and chairs. We also dug out our Honda generator and solar panel, which were connected to a car battery, so we could charge our electrical equipment. There was a vast array of battery chargers that turned into a bird's nest of wires. Unhappily the generator proved unreliable. Every day one of us would tinker with it, cleaning spark plugs or fuel lines to get the thing to work for an hour or two.

We then dug a latrine away from Base Camp over a small moraine ridge and pitched a small tent over the hole for privacy and shelter. With the communal area sorted, each of us put up his or her own personal tent. It was essential to have our own space, somewhere we could put out all our gear and begin to prepare for the climb. Finally we were finished and could eat.

Base Camp was still rudimentary, but I knew that over the following days we would improve it, making it into a comfortable space where we could relax and recover. The simplicity of the mountains was seeping back into me. Norman Collie put it very well: 'The sense of freedom, of perfect contentment with our present lot, blessed gift of the mountains to their true and faithful devotees, was beginning to steal over us. Languidly, we talked about the morrow, our only regret arising from our inability to catch a glimpse of that monarch of the mountains, Nanga Parbat and the ice-fringed precipices which overhang his southern face.'

Sleep came easily that night.

PART 2
MAZENO

PART 2
MAZENO

04

THE DIVIDING LINE

Doug Scott had a lot of bad luck on the Mazeno Ridge. On his first attempt, during a hot dry summer in August 1992, rock fall badly injured his teammate Valeri Pershin while he was placing supplies at the Mazeno Gap. Pershin was swept eighty metres, leaving him badly cut and with several broken ribs. It says a lot about his Russian stoicism that he remained at Base Camp to recover, while Doug, Sergey Efimov and Ang Phurba Sherpa established a base camp below the Mazeno Pass at the western end of the ridge. Next day they climbed ice and snow to a subsidiary peak at 6,650 metres and then went over the first of the Mazeno Ridge's summits – Point 6,880m – before camping on a saddle on its far side. Yet now the wind strengthened and Ang Phurba, complaining of injuries sustained on the dangerous Schell route, decided he could go no further.

Doug returned in 1993 with a small team but was avalanched while acclimatising on a nearby mountain, badly damaging his ankle. He had to be carried out on the back of a horse and the expedition didn't set foot on the Mazeno Ridge. Rick and I were part of Doug's final attempt on the ridge in July 1995, along with the Polish genius Voytek Kurtyka and our Australian friend Andrew Lock. This time there was no thought of leaving supplies at the Mazeno Gap or acclimatising on other peaks. We would acclimatise on the ridge itself, making a couple of forays to dump loads at the start of the ridge. Unusually bad monsoon weather was predicted and we felt it best to get on with things.

On 2 August we climbed back up to a pinnacle at 5,650 metres, where we'd cached some gear, and continued. Voytek mispronounced the word pinnacle as 'pineapple', and after that the pineapple became a landmark on the ridge. He and I were soloing out in front unroped; we seemed to be waiting ages for the others. Sheltering out of the wind, Voytek and I discussed this. I wasn't happy we were losing so much time, but I was also aware that if anyone needed to take his time gaining altitude that it was me. Now in my late thirties, I knew very well I was slow to acclimatise. As it turned out, Doug was ill. We were all a bit shocked; Doug was always the superpower of our expeditions – our main man.

We camped above the pineapple that night but had already decided to retreat in the morning as the weather was deteriorating. Back at Base Camp the bad weather continued and we spent some time hanging out. Rick, Doug and our Pakistani liaison officer Abdul Quadir took a walk up to the Mazeno Pass at 5,399 metres. The rest of us pottered about sorting out equipment, reading and lifting boulders as a keep-fit exercise. When Doug got back from the Mazeno Pass he told us he'd decided to leave the expedition. It was a great disappointment. We still weren't sure what was wrong with him but thought he had heat stroke or was simply tired out from his usual frenetic schedule. Perhaps our bike ride hadn't been such a good idea? Doug was soon in Islamabad, laid up in bed suffering from what turned out to be severe gastroenteritis.

I was really upset by Doug's departure. It was a strange feeling; up to that point I hadn't really been aware how much his companionship mattered to me. I was growing close to Voytek and we shared a similar, almost spiritual, discipline about climbing and living. Rick was an old friend and I got on well with Andrew. I tried to reason with myself, to figure out why I was not focused on the climb. I slept fitfully at Base Camp and all the time my thoughts were with Doug. The weather remained poor, and coming down from a foray on to the ridge I decided I should also retire from the climb and go home. I eventually caught up with Doug as we arrived at Rawalpindi airport to check in for our departure flights.

Rick, Voytek and Andrew stayed to make further forays along the ridge to the 'point of no return'. They told me that to climb down and along that convoluted part of the ridge was the moment you became totally committed to the climb and to reaching the Mazeno Gap. It meant stepping through a door that locked behind you. I began to wonder how you would manage to climb the Mazeno in a good style and get home safely. Turning the problem over in my mind, the ridge seemed incredibly dangerous. Voytek went back with Erhard Loretan in 1997 and I might have joined them if I hadn't been going through a personal crisis that resulted ultimately in the end of my marriage. Bad weather meant they didn't reach the previous high point.

It seemed no coincidence to me that the two teams that had done best on the ridge – the Americans in 2004 and the Germans four years later – had set off along the ridge fit and acclimatised from other climbs. Even so, they hadn't had the energy and resources to press on to the summit. They had both faced difficult descents, the Americans down the Schell and the Germans down the Diamir Face, following a dangerous route Messner had used when he soloed the mountain. Clearly the line between being prepared and being too tired and run down from altitude was a fine one.

Still, the effort by Steve Swenson and Doug Chabot in particular had inspired me to commit to trying this route again. The ridge could be climbed. All I had to do was to come up with a plan to get some climbers along the ridge and still have the energy left to allow those who could to continue to the summit. At that stage I had little idea how I could do that when climbing in pure alpine style. I wasn't interested in fixing a banister of fixed rope up the route. Rick and I had committed to trying again in 2010, but my chaotic finances got in the way. It was only with Cathy coming on board that we had the resources to try.

Our ideas, endlessly discussed and finely drawn, like all plans of battle, didn't survive for long in the face of the enemy. Thanks to the deep winter snow, our plan of starting on the Diamir Face had been abandoned. But we still needed to acclimatise. Time was tight, so we would simply have to get on with it as best we could. Rick and I knew this meant we would acclimatise on the initial ridge above Base Camp that led up to the Mazeno from the south; but it wasn't something I wanted to do. Many high-altitude climbers wouldn't think twice about it; they would follow other teams up the same mountain on a well-compacted trail and it wouldn't even occur to them that there were any ethical consi-derations. I have to compromise when I'm working as a guide, but in my own climbing, I try to maintain a high sense of ethics; on all my private climbing expeditions I want to make our attempt as close to alpine style as is possible. This expedition to Nanga Parbat was no different in that respect. So we wondered how we could acclimatise without risking our pure definition of an alpine-style ascent.

There were some nice mountains of around 6,000 metres relatively close to Base Camp that we could have climbed, but as soon as we arrived we saw they were carrying huge amounts of snow. The avalanche risk seemed high. I didn't want to end our expedition while acclimatising, as Doug had in 1993. Neither Rick nor I had seen so much snow at Base Camp before, and it became obvious there was no real alternative to breaking trail on the climb up to the Mazeno.

After a night at Base Camp, Cathy, Rick and I took a walk up a steep rocky peak just above Base Camp, from where we spied an interesting line up to a subsidiary ridge that led in turn to the Mazeno itself. This was to the left of the line Doug had shown us in 1995. His route took us to the same ridge, but, while it was safe, it followed a big semi-circular arc to get there. With more snow on the mountain, we decided to go for the steeper, more direct route. I had concerns about avalanches, but there was a rock rib going up the slope and I reckoned that this rib would give us adequate protection and keep us safe. On 17 June we all went on the mountain for the first time, pitching a store tent at the top of a col at 5,650 metres before descending to Base Camp to rest for the night.

All this work was good for my acclimatisation, but the three Lhakpas were already perfectly happy in the thin air, having just come in from Nepal. They had recently been on the summits of either Everest or Kangchenjunga, and were moving much faster than us. I suggested they sort their gear and hang out – enjoy a few days off while Cathy, Rick and I made efforts to catch up with them. I warned them that once we had caught up with our own acclimatisation we would all be really busy. They should enjoy the rest because it wasn't going to last.

At first the Sherpas were happy to do nothing and it was interesting to see them bouldering two days later as we came down from our first night on the hill, at 5,650 metres. Normally on expeditions it's the Western climbers who are bouldering and languishing around Base Camp while the Sherpas are hard at work on the mountain. Yet even with all their base-camp activities the Lhakpas soon became stir crazy. Rangdu said: 'Hey, Mr Sandy, can we fix ropes up to the col as you guys are going up and down it all the time? We may as well do something!'

I pondered his request. It really was a problem for me, as I'd had no intention of using fixed ropes at all, even though we'd brought some just in case, but it made sense. Each day the sun softened the snow and small slides of snow threatened the ridge as the day wore on. The three of us Western climbers needed to keep going up and down several more times to get our bodies used to the thin air and the risk we were taking seemed pointless. So after talking it through with Cathy and Rick, we agreed to let them fix. The Sherpas were delighted to have a role. No more sitting around Base Camp for them. Next day, the three Lhakpas fixed rope, while Cathy, Rick and I were able to go higher, knowing that the ropes were there behind us to speed our descent.

Soon we had put up an old dome tent at 6,150 metres – Camp 1 – and were able to make forays higher up the mountain. Bad weather and regular snowfall meant the trail had to be broken again and again. Climbing above this camp, we were often fearful of avalanches, and at one point I went ahead suggesting the others spread further apart so we didn't overload the slope. I had to call on all my years of avalanche training to judge the fine line between being cautious and pressing on. While the snow was deep, it held firm. I traversed out to an easier-angled but less direct route up the slope rather than taking the line of steps we had broken the day before, which was now almost obscured by fresh snow. We all knew we were pushing too hard. I dug a snow test pit to assess how well the different layers of snow were bonded together. The snow pack seemed to be averagely bonded, yet I still felt we were trading close to the edge. I knew I was being influenced by the urge to get high and acclimatised. We couldn't afford the luxury of lying around at Base Camp letting the season drift away. Anyway, the Sherpas were pacing round Base Camp like racehorses waiting for the off, waiting for us to catch up. We climbed on.

It's an easy trap to fall into, experienced climbers pushing on and on, closing their minds to the obvious signs below their feet. But the line I took finally got us off the slope, which eased back and led us, after several hundred metres, to a whaleback false summit being blasted by strong winds. In its lee we decided to pitch one of our little bivvy tents – Camp 2. The altitude was 6,400 metres. In a stroke of good luck, the snow now stopped falling, the view cleared and, while a cold wind was still blowing the snow around, we felt happy and quite proud to be that high. It had been only eight days since we arrived at Base Camp, and here we were, already at 6,400 metres, feeling weak but otherwise fine.

We descended to Base Camp to rest for a couple of days and then the three of us went back up, pitched another of the bivvy tents and spent a night at Camp 2. The next day, 27 June, we descended once more to Base Camp, dismantling the storage tent we'd put up at 5,650 metres on the way. In the meantime, the three

Lhakpas carried supplies up to our high point of 6,400 metres. Our night in the bivvy tents had left all of us feeling tired and as we descended we agreed that ideally we would rest, come up and spend another night at that altitude and then go down to Base Camp again. Then we would rest some more and only then start our attempt on the ridge. Now that the vast scale of the challenge was firmly in front of us, it seemed incredibly imposing. We felt weeks away from our attempt.

When we got back to the tents, the weather forecast made us think again. While researching the expedition, Rick had been in touch with the Met Office in Bracknell and told the forecasters we were looking for a week of good weather on Nanga Parbat. They got back to him after a week and told him their records suggested that this never happened. Now we had a forecast that looked too good to miss. We were promised five days of good weather followed by a storm. We knew full well we were bound to get a storm at some point. The ridge was so long there was no way we could avoid one. It was also likely that when it happened we would be caught somewhere that was incredibly exposed. That was just the reality of committing to such an extended adventure.

The promise of five days of good weather on Nanga Parbat, the killer mountain, seemed too good to waste on further acclimatisation. We discussed the pros and cons of getting back on the mountain immediately so as to take advantage of it. I feared the prospect of being stuck in a tent at 7,000 metres on a knife-edge ridge, but if we were realistic about climbing this route we had to accept the risk. We had known all along that in all likelihood we would have to face that situation. So we made the decision that after two or three nights' rest we would all head back up, spend a night at Camp 1, climb back up to the bivvy tents at 6,400 metres and, the following morning, go for it as a team of six for a full-hearted attempt on the Mazeno Ridge.

And so, on the morning of 4 July, I woke at 6,400 metres on the third day of our climb. I could tell the sun wasn't shining, and it was still bitterly cold. Hoar frost coated the inside of the single-skinned bivouac tent. I turned the stove on to start melting snow for drinks and porridge. Next to me in the tent was Cathy. Rangdu and Rick shared another, while Zarok and Nuru were together in the third tent. Moving carefully to stop the frost from sprinkling over our sleeping bags and gear, we finished our porridge and biscuits and started packing. Finally we stuffed our feet back into our boots and left our warm cocoon, reversing out of the tent's narrow door to greet the day.

I took in a lungful of cold pure air and looked around. The sky was turning blue and I could see for miles, the mountains towering around our perch at 6,400 metres. This was the springboard for our great adventure. As the sun broke the horizon and lit up the tent's orange fabric, we dismantled the poles and packed them away. I stared in a kind of numb horror at the amount of equipment we needed to carry. There seemed to be tons of it. We had all our personal clothing for the whole climb, then a shell and down insulation. Some of us were already in down suits. We had a few pairs of spare socks, vital for staving off frostbite. There were cameras, head torches, spare batteries, thirty-two gas cylinders, three stoves with pots and pans, drinking bowls and basic cutlery. We had around twenty-five kilograms of food between the six of us. There were the three 50-metre dynamic climbing ropes, a spare abseil rope we could abandon as needed and a small rack of ice screws, pitons and wired nuts, along with a few quickdraws and some tape slings with karabiners. We also had a fifty-metre length of thinner line to cut up into lengths for abseil anchors and secure our tents if necessary. If there was any left, it would be useful as a lightweight climbing rope on the summit push.

The abseil rope I expected to carry to our 1995 point of no return. We would fix it and leave it hanging there in case we had to reverse the ridge in the face of bad weather or injury. Climbing a vertical wall like that in a state of exhaustion and perhaps with broken limbs would be too much. We were constantly aware that once committed to the ridge, we were only leaving it at one of its two ends. There was no other escape. I felt a little fearful, packing our stuff away, but I appreciated that feeling; it engenders respect, and that is healthy. The fear was manageable; if it wasn't, I wouldn't have been there.

Our sacks felt heavy – too heavy for climbing. Cathy's sack looked a bit less bulky, but I knew it was just as heavy as mine. As our communications expert she carried the satellite phone and a small, handheld computer with spare batteries. She would use these to send text messages and occasional photos to Twitter and Facebook. She was also in charge of collecting our all-important weather forecasts, something we could never have dreamed of in the mid 1990s.

Our twenty-five kilograms of food should last about eight days but, if we rationed it, we could probably spin that out to ten. I don't like chemical foods like gels and protein bars; I'd rather have something more organic. I find porridge, oatcakes, digestive biscuits and peanut butter, with the occasional tin of tuna or some other fish, will keep me going for long periods. I like the taste and texture as I eat them, and appetite is often a problem at altitude. Rick, on the other hand, seems to like gels, and many nutritionists will disagree with me. Astronauts seem to use these kinds of foods for long periods without any ill effects, but I find them excessively sweet, and find sucking gel out of foil wrappers revolting at sea level, let alone at 7,000 metres. My body does just fine eking out my frugal rations without resorting to squeezing disgustingly sweet refined sugars into my mouth. Gels also leave me thirsty and more often than not I puke them up anyway. They might be fine for a day or two but trying to survive on energy foods for eight to ten days would be difficult for me. I am sure my intestines would pack up.

We divided ourselves into three teams of two, with a climbing rope per team. Cathy climbed with Rangdu, and Nuru teamed up with Zarok while Rick and I roped together. Although we divided in this way, the plan was to stay close together and work for each other. I thought about the ridge ahead and all those summits over 7,000 metres. I thought about Doug Chabot and Steve Swenson. How hard was the climbing really? I told myself to stay cool and relax, to control my emotions and enjoy each minute as it slipped past. Those minutes would become hours soon enough, the hours would turn to days and each freezing night would give way to another new morning. I told myself to enjoy them and live for the moment.

And so we began this impeccable ridge.

Nuru was in front at first, breaking trail slightly downhill from our camp. I looked behind us and saw that only our footsteps remained. Then we traversed a steep wall of snow that turned out to be soft and Nuru's legs sank in deep. Following in his tracks, we did the same. It was hard work for everyone, and above us the slope continued to rise. We hardly stopped at all, keeping a steady pace – guide's pace we call it – slow but steady wins the race. It's a pace I can keep all day and all night if necessary. I thought about my days as a teenager, the Scottish school holidays coming to an end, and the Glorious Twelfth of August in the Highlands. Grouse beating gave me the chance to earn some extra pocket money.

Walking the hills of the Haughs of Cromdale, Dorback and the Kinveachy, a line of school kids and impoverished students waved white cotton flags secured to branches pruned from saplings, scaring – or more officially 'driving' – grouse so they would fly over foreigners' guns and be shot. Black Labradors, springer spaniels and Irish red setters would collect the shot birds, which were of more value to the shooters than us country peasants. My twin brother and I could gallop over the hills at an impressive rate and a friendly old gamekeeper called Charlie Oswald used to shout at us: 'Boys, if you run in the morning you'll be exhausted by night!' The last drive would come and as we made our way back to the vehicles that used to take us home, we would run by old Charlie the gamekeeper, laughing and shouting as we passed him: 'That's right Charlie, if you run in the morning … '

Now I was here, pacing myself on this huge climb, thinking ahead and plotting campsites with some shelter from the wind, flattish areas where we could avoid too much digging and pitch our bivvy tents with minimal effort. We needed to rest properly and conserve our energy for the next day, and the one after that, and after that … Our initial acclimatisation plan might not have survived, but this one was working well. We came to a good spot at 6,800 metres, a whaleback sort of ridge in a small col.

Tents sprouted like mushrooms from the snow, with hardly a word. Speaking seemed unnecessary. Automatically, one team-member crawled inside each tent, three stoves ignited, almost in unison, and the first pans of snow were put on to melt. Hydration was everything. We fought thirst constantly as the thin dry air sucked the moisture out of our bodies.

The next day – 5 July – went well and we made good progress. We were now on the ridge proper, looking down on to the Diamir Glacier some two and a half kilometres below us. We could see groups of tents at the Diamir Base Camp. It encouraged us to think that other groups would be climbing on the Kinshofer route. If we came down that way, we might find some friendly faces to help us along. The altitude now was between 6,800 and 7,000 metres. It was colder than expected, but as long as I could keep moving I was warm enough in just my Power Stretch trousers, with a breathable top and my down jacket. The others preferred to wear their down clothing all the time.

Looking ahead, the length of the ridge seemed almost inconceivable. The Sherpas realised now that what I had told them was true, although they still thought we could knock it off in six days. We were enjoying the exposed ridge, but the snow was now deep and unconsolidated. It was exhausting work. We arrived at steeper ground, exposed and technical. Nuru was in front again and was forced out on to a very steep mixed wall of rock and snow. As he attempted to wade across past a steep rock gendarme, his footsteps in the unreliable snow gave way under him. He fell and accelerated down the slope. I shouted to Zarok to watch the rope but he was too close to Nuru and there was lots of slack between them. The rope continued to run out as Nuru fell and I wondered if Zarok would be catapulted out of his footsteps when it finally came tight.

Startled into action, Zarok got a grip of the rope and Nuru finally stopped. I looked at the line of his fall; it was clear of any rocks so it was unlikely that he would be badly injured. Unless there was some obstruction hidden below the surface of the snow, I thought he'd probably be fine. Even so, it would have been easy to catch a crampon point on a patch of ice and twist an ankle or knee. Half buried in snow, Nuru stood up, shook himself down and looked around. His movements seemed clumsy and slow. At first I thought he had hurt himself, but it soon became obvious that the weight of his rucksack and the soft unconsolidated snow were making things difficult for him. He was fine.

Zarok held the rope tight and Nuru tried to climb up, but it was hopeless in the deep snow. We moved towards him and eventually climbed down to help. Having regrouped, we looked around. We had been forced on to very steep and avalanche-prone ground and so traversed to a rock wall where I found a tiny loop of old accessory cord threaded into a crack. It was a sure sign that one of the other teams had come this way. I looked up; they had probably abseiled from the steeper gendarmes of the knife-edge ridge above and then had most likely continued abseiling from this thread into the couloir below.

My first thought was to do the same and abseil lower. After that we could move around the stubby rock spurs below. It looked straightforward enough, but I could see that the area was filled with unconsolidated snow. So while it looked the easiest line,

I decided to traverse and not risk it. Rangdu searched my eyes for direction and I gestured back towards the knife-edge ridge. Even though the climbing was technical and exposed, sticking to the rock would minimise the avalanche risk, avoid height loss and keep us as close to the ridge as reasonably possible.

Progress was necessarily quite slow and as darkness came we realised we were not going to reach a comfortable bivouac site. I made the call to stop when we came to a small ledge with bivvy potential. By now it was almost dark; this was safest and best, I told myself. I knew a bad night out at this stage would really weaken us and I was incredibly concerned. I sensed this could be the unfortunate event that might really tire us out. From our earliest planning, this was always my main concern. If we became exhausted early on, how would we ever keep going just to reach the Mazeno Gap?

Looking ahead was difficult – the view was obscured by steep rock and various small pinnacles, all shrouded with deep unconsolidated snow. We got some pegs into a crack and fixed a tensioned rope between them. Once we were all clipped in to that, it felt a bit safer. I started to hack at the rock ledge and some of the loose stuff came off. Rangdu, Cathy and I rolled a big boulder out of the way and made enough room to half-erect one of the bivvy tents. Rick was working away at the other end of the ledge in a letterbox-type feature. He managed to excavate a shelter from the snow and rock that was shaped like a coffin for two corpses.

Between these two platforms there was a flattish ledge and with further digging, like a dentist hacking at an old filling, we levered out some loose rotten rock and expanded the platform. It wasn't quite wide enough to pitch a tent but was big enough for two people to bivvy side by side. I urged everyone – quite unnecessarily – to make themselves as comfortable as possible. All seemed happy with the places they had chosen; we all knew it was far from ideal but we would cope.

I gingerly climbed away from the safety line, filled a bag with snow and then moved into the precariously pitched bivvy tent. The drop below our campsite was very steep; anything falling would go straight down to the Diamir Glacier thousands of metres below. Cathy was inside not feeling very well but she was positive and chatty. We were all a bit shaken having seen Nuru fall, and the tricky climbing afterwards with heavy rucksacks hadn't helped.

The worry of finding a suitable space to spend the night had preyed on my mind. I was the leader and our plans seemed to be falling into disarray. I appreciated being inside the tent and out of the freezing temperatures; for the others, I knew, it would be a cold night. Inside the tent, Cathy and I would benefit a little from the heat of our very efficient stove. Most of the energy would go into the pan, but some would escape into our confined space. The other four would not have this luxury.

Through the tent flap I could see Rick and Rangdu's feet wrapped in sleeping bags, and tent fabric sticking out of the bottom of their rock and snow shelter. Nuru and Zarok were inside their sleeping bags and inside their bivvy tent without the poles, using it as a big survival bag. Rangdu told Rick the next day that he had never had to cope with a forced bivvy in the high mountains before; he had worked on high-altitude commercial expeditions where camping was planned, with good tents pitched on carefully selected camping spots and with the best possible food and lots of cooking gas to melt snow and quench their high-altitude thirsts.

By now all of us had our stoves going and were melting water, so that was a positive. I closed the zip of the tent and snuggled into my sleeping bag. The stoves burned late into the night and then fell silent as we finally tried to sleep. Mountain Equipment had given us all sleeping bags with Gore-Tex outers, so that was a plus. They wouldn't get damp, no matter where we slept. Equipment had changed since my first forays in the Alps: fabrics were lighter and more protective; insulation was lighter and warmer; stoves were much more efficient and yet they too were lighter. For years I've passed on design suggestions to Mountain Equipment, who have supported me with gear for much of my career. One of the reasons such huge undertakings in the Himalaya are now becoming possible is because of design expertise and rapid improvements in outdoor equipment materials and technologies. Climbing hard for ten days at extreme altitude in alpine style was only conceivable because of such developments.

Cathy rustled beside me, jarring me awake a few times. At one point she vomited and I grew concerned for her; what if the melted snow was contaminated in some way?

Years ago Cathy and I had climbed Lhotse together. I had been curious enough to want to reach the summit of Lhotse West before going on to the main summit. I was soloing, although in reality climbing alone was more accurate. Nowadays in the Western Cwm you can't really solo because there are literally hundreds of people trying to climb Mount Everest. I was the first to try Lhotse that season and once I left the main track it was much harder going, breaking trail by myself. I had tried to get high on Lhotse but the snow was so deep that I turned back a few hundred metres above the 'Turtle', an exposed rock that forms a small island in the surrounding snow.

I was quite disappointed by this failure and was feeling a bit dejected; I had been hanging about the Western Cwm for a while and felt I was getting nowhere. On the way down I met Cathy. While we had met before we had never climbed together. During this unexpected meeting high in the Western Cwm, I told her how disappointed I was, explaining that the snow was deep and there was no way I could break trail all by myself up the steep couloir to the summit. I told her I was thinking of abandoning my climb. She told me she was climbing with Pemba Tengin Sherpa and I could team up with them if I wished. I had met Pemba several times before, so I was delighted at Cathy's suggestion.

I was out in front breaking trail at the top of the couloir, when I decided on a whim that I would traverse out to the right and check out the summit there rather than turn left to the top of Lhotse's official main summit. The reason I suppose arose from a small article in a climbing magazine suggesting that Lhotse's west summit was actually higher. Some accompanying photos taken from various angles showed that this might well be the case. So, I climbed up some steep loose rock, which was quite awkward, and looking back down I saw Cathy following me. I offered to throw down a rope. She tied on and continued up. Some of the sections were loose and awkward so I was pleased to be roped up.

Pemba decided not to bother and instead headed up to Lhotse's main summit, which turned out to be a wise move. I continued up the rock and Cathy watched the ropes. Not long afterwards we came to a cairn with some very old prayer flags wrapped around it and I climbed on to the exposed ridge. Even as a climber, used to such places, I felt precariously balanced. Cathy just stood on the ridge, telling me that she was not moving from that lonely and unfriendly spot.

I asked Cathy to watch my ropes and, with lots of slack, scrambled and climbed along the crest and came back on to a pinnacle. We took some photos but it was misty and unpleasant. On the summit I lay on my tummy and looked over the south face of Lhotse and thought: 'Holy hell, that's wild and steep.' I wondered if Tomo Česen really had climbed it or if the story of him making it all up was accurate. I thought: 'If he really did this then he must have wings on his ankles.' I thought also of Jerzy Kukuczka, the second man after Reinhold Messner to climb the fourteen 8,000-metre peaks. Jerzy was climbing a fixed rope just six millimetres thick on this face at 8,200 metres, not far from where I was now, when it broke and he fell to his death. Kukuczka was one of my great heroes. Unlike Messner, he had come from a poor country and had to hustle his way to the big mountains, coming up with clever schemes to smuggle goods to pay for it all. There was no doubt in my mind that Jerzy Kukuczka was outstanding.

I climbed back to Cathy and put the rope around some sound rock so we could abseil back to easy ground. By now Pemba was back from the main summit. It hadn't taken him long. The mist had closed in and the wind was howling. He and Cathy spoke while I coiled the rope and then Cathy shouted over the noise of the wind that they were going down. As the weather was deteriorating I thought I had better go down too. The main summit would have been cool and I was sure I'd be back. I wanted to spy out a route to Lhotse Middle, another neighbouring summit that was said to be the highest unclimbed point in the world. Mal Duff and I had looked at it many years before, another obsession just like the Mazeno.

I have no explanation for why I am drawn to climb new things, except that it's fun. Girlfriends and journalists who try to peer inside my empty head tell me it's ego, or competition with other men. The boring truth is that I just like exploring. As a kid I was always rolling big stones over to find out what insects lay beneath. If my dad gave me his pen, within seconds I would have taken it apart to see how it worked, usually dropping vital parts on the floor. I'd usually end up with a smacked backside for my curiosity.

Cathy and I became good friends after Lhotse, and that's why she was here now, vomiting and rustling in her sleep on a tiny ledge part way along the Mazeno Ridge. I knew that she was strong, even though she hadn't expected to get all the way on the Mazeno. But this forced bivouac was a serious setback and I hoped she'd get through it.

In the morning we were alive and still in reasonable shape. There were no frozen body parts and we all busily melted snow, but our situation was uncomfortable and we all wanted to get out of there as quickly as possible. Once we traversed and climbed the rock walls ahead we were bound to find a better place to rest. We had a quick drink and something to eat and packed up.

The climbing turned out to be quite awkward, up steep rock walls with ledges covered in soft, light snow that complicated the climbing further. After several hours we came to a small but sheltered col where a cold wind was blowing mist across the mountain tops. We decided to put up the tents and get the stoves on to melt snow. It had been a short day but everyone was tired – we could have pushed on, but none of us knew what lay ahead or whether we'd find a better place to camp. The decision was an obvious one.

The problem was that rocks and cornices enclosed our small site, blocking the satellite phone signal. The following day was predicted to be when the storm hit, but now we couldn't check. Looking at the cloud formations around us, the message was clear: the winds were going to strengthen. At least our camping spot was flat and protected. We battened down the hatches and prepared to wait, but with no idea for how long. A day? A week? And all the time we would be eating up our store of food.

The following day was windy enough, but it wasn't the wildness I expected. Still, it would have been nasty going, so I was glad of the chance to recuperate. We had lots of gas. But we had been on the ridge for five days now, and we were still only halfway to the Mazeno Gap with the hardest climbing yet to come.

05

MIND THE GAP

The following day was much less windy but the snow was still deep. We climbed on over sections of rock and snow, one peak followed by another, and then another. The exposure was immense but I loved being there. It was a traverse in the heavens, our world dropping steeply away on either side and then spreading out to views of distant peaks beyond. The ridge wound sinuously like a serpent's coils, decorated with steeply curved cornices poised like frozen waves. Time was stretching out in either direction too. There seemed to be nothing before or after this ridge.

Now we came to a steep gap – our point of no return. We deliberated what to do. It was straightforward enough to cut some of the thin cord and pass it around some rocks and tie a loop. We threaded the abseil rope through this anchor and joined it to one of the fifty-metre climbing ropes before tossing them down into the void. Then I clipped in and slid down the rope. I felt as though I was walking in space, my heavy rucksack tipping me backwards, leaving me feeling cumbersome and disoriented.

Rangdu and I were first down. We climbed across to a snow bank and easier ground, where we fixed the other end of the rope. One by one, the others followed, their crampons scratching and sparking on the rock, before scrambling across to where we waited so they could detach themselves from the rope. The wind howled and stung our faces as we waited patiently for everyone to regroup. Then, as the others climbed onwards, I pulled the climbing rope and left the abseil rope behind.

It was a slender thread of safety. I knew full well that if something went wrong in the next few days we might be forced to come back this way and climb up this blank rock wall. It would be a dreadful predicament if one of us was injured midway between here and the Mazeno Gap and we had to decide which way to go to get back to safety. Retracing our steps would not be easy, but the alternative of pushing on might be impossible. The thought of retreat was unnerving; we would be in a desperate state to make that choice. But there were only three options: press on to the Mazeno Gap, go back the way we'd come or sit on the ridge and freeze to death. Were we now in a place of no return? Had we, with that abseil, totally committed ourselves to getting to the Mazeno Gap? I thought of the climbers who had been here before us, so strong and fast. 'Ooh la la,' I thought to myself, 'what am I leading us into?' I looked ahead and saw the others tramping along the ridge in front of me, pushing on, dancing along a pathway in the sky which at any moment might become a mantrap. At least right now all was going well. That's as much as any of us can hope for.

The next bivvy was fine but I found myself growing fractious with my tent-mate. It was a silly, tiny thing. At night as we finished melting snow and arranged our equipment before going to sleep, Cathy would take her rucksack and place it over the stove and pots in the doorway of our bivvy tent. This scuppered my system for waking up in the morning and reaching easily for the stove. One of us had to move her rucksack out of the way first, and this brought a cascade of hoar frost down on to our sleeping bags, where it thawed, making them damp.

It also meant whoever lit the stove had to get half out of their sleeping bag. Normally I could do this lying down, so I could remain in a doze, slowly waking up while the water took its time to boil. Why couldn't she use her rucksack as a pillow like the rest of us? I realise sitting here at my desk in the comfort of my warm home how pathetic this sounds. Such frustrations are part of life at high altitude and I tried not to say anything about it. But it drove me nuts at the time. I wonder what I was doing that did the same to her.

That morning – 9 July – started with the usual shower of hoar frost, lighting the stove and struggling into my clothes. It was already 7 a.m. – quite a lie-in. I seem to have amazing circulation and during the night get warmer and warmer, so that I actually have to take clothes off. First thing in the morning, when I start moving, I need to cover my skin quickly. We made drinks and some porridge and then exited the tent. By this stage of the climb, after a week on the ridge, the others simply assumed we would be the last to be ready and as usual we were.

This annoyed me slightly but I couldn't put that down to Cathy's rucksack routine. The truth is that I love hanging out in my sleeping bag first thing in the morning. Anyway, we were only a few minutes behind the others, and somebody had to be last. Everyone else was busy striking tents or having a pee and barely noticed that we were fractionally behind. It's of no consequence, so why did I care? Why was I on edge? As we packed up, I sang – badly – a Chuck Berry song, School Day. Then I thought: 'I must be hard to share a tent with really.' The sacks were packed, and we were underway again. For a group of six we were actually very efficient.

That day we crossed Mazeno Peak, the highest of the 7,000-metre peaks. The maps told us the height was 7,120 metres, but our altimeters weren't so generous, registering not much more than 7,000 metres. After a week's climbing, none of us had much faith that the altimeters were working correctly, but then again, our weather forecast, arriving from a meteorologist in Andorra, had predicted stronger winds and snow for that day, so it was possible the pressure was dropping. That would affect the altimeters. With the prospect of bad weather and the knowledge that the pinnacles, the crux of the route, were now just ahead of us, we decided to stop early at 1 p.m. and get a good rest.

I had no desire to be out on the ridge in bad weather. Earlier, in similar conditions, I had felt a weird itching under my hat as I climbed along behind Rick and the Lhakpas. I scratched my head, thinking it was time to comb my hair to try and clean it a bit. And then it dawned on me that what I was feeling was static electricity crawling across my scalp. All of us felt it, but no one mentioned it until we'd moved a few hundred metres further along the ridge. We had become inured to such things. We would accept our fate.

The next morning we found ourselves grinding slowly through the pinnacles. The rocks were covered in puffy, unconsolidated snow, making progress difficult. The Sherpas had assumed we would cruise through this section but, not for the first time, they had underestimated the twists and turns of this incredible and apparently never-ending ridge. They had thought we would be through to the Mazeno Gap in six days; we were now on day nine. I had found myself trying to dampen their optimism: 'No guys, we are carrying tons of gear and the snow conditions are bad. We are here for the long haul – expect nothing and we may be pleased with progress. Live simply, take it one day at a time.'

I was becoming more Buddhist than the Sherpas themselves. During the initial phase of the expedition I had taken ages to acclimatise compared to Rick and Cathy, and felt I was often behind. I had really thought it would be impossible for me to keep up and that I would be unlikely to make it. So I cooled my ambition and resorted to a mantra – one step at a time and let's just see what happens.

The climbing was getting harder and, while we were making progress, we were moving too slowly. At times we fixed our ropes in a kind of capsule style, with the last climber stripping the gear as he followed, just to keep us moving a bit faster. I knew that the Americans had been through here in about eleven hours and from the few photos they published with their report it seemed that they had more consolidated snow on their traverse than the froth we were obliged to wade through. As time passed I could see frustration building in the Sherpas; we would get glimpses towards the summit ridge of Nanga Parbat and could see that it still looked a long way off. The three Lhakpas and Cathy were becoming a little exasperated by it all.

We had to abseil down a tricky section and then traverse a very sharp ridge to some more abseils. At times it was around Scottish grade IV, but, with the complication of high altitude, grades seem meaningless. Searching for suitable anchor points was not always easy on rock that was quite broken, and while pulling the ropes afterwards they brought down a shower of loose stones. Happily, it was only the ones wearing helmets who got struck on the head. Sometimes the ropes stuck a little, and we'd panic, but they never jammed completely. On one 50-metre abseil we found a piece of tat, a small human reminder that someone had been this way before.

Finally, as the sun was setting and we climbed in the pink evening light, we came to a point that we knew was very close to the Mazeno Gap. After eleven hours on the go we had done it. We cleared an obvious site to camp knowing that we were just a few hundred metres of easy ground short of our first big goal. That evening we felt relieved and delighted – we were finally there. All the team were still together and Cathy had become the first woman to traverse the ridge. Ten people in total had now reached this point, six of them on our expedition. We felt elated; an important milestone had been reached and as we drank and ate inside our tents we all felt very pleased with ourselves.

The next morning, 11 July, we woke late after the trials of the previous day – at 8 a.m. The reality of our situation now became clearer. It was our tenth day on the route. In planning the climb, I'd thought that the Mazeno Gap would be a smart place to rest up for a day. The altitude is around 6,940 metres and, I imagined, we would have been on the hill for six to eight days by this stage. Our tired bodies would be glad of a rest day and the spare time would allow us to melt snow and get properly hydrated. Now that we were actually there our food supply was getting sparse; none of us had enjoyed a proper meal since leaving Base Camp. Thanks to the altitude and the strain of climbing, we were probably burning something like five to six thousand calories a day. We had already had a rest day, forced on us by the forecast of bad weather. The truth was that we didn't have enough supplies, apart from gas canisters, or the physical reserves to hang around. On top of that, the weather was perfect.

Without much conviction, I mentioned the idea of resting up for a day anyway. It occurred to me that one of the team might have been looking forward to stopping for a bit and hanging out in this wonderful place. All three Lhakpas, Rick and Cathy made it perfectly clear that they were keener to push on; we couldn't let this good weather slip through our fingers. Without further discussion we struck the tents and packed up; we were on our way again at 10.30 a.m., climbing down to the Mazeno Gap proper before starting the climb back uphill, turning some pinnacles on the Rupal side of the face, to our right-hand side as we faced the summit.

It was much harder going steeply uphill and I did wonder if, in our enthusiasm and excitement at having achieved so much, we had given adequate consideration to the state of our bodies. Perhaps we should have taken a rest day? As we climbed we talked a little and decided we could always take a rest at the next bivvy site if we felt we really needed it, although the lack of supplies made that unlikely. We all seemed to be feeling positive in our three teams of two. The weather was sunny and the climbing absorbing, with some tricky traverses and a steep gully of soft unconsolidated snow that felt difficult at that altitude.

Finally, we came to a scree slope that curved upwards into a small flat plateau at about 7,160 metres. There was now a slight breeze and, since the spot looked so accommodating, we decided to camp at around 2.30 p.m. We took our time moving some boulders and lumps of rock to get level platforms – hard and mundane work at high altitude – and then secured the tents with stones. We fully expected the winds to strengthen sooner rather than later.

Having camped on rock, we were able to sit in the afternoon sunshine on boulders outside the tents, chatting together as a group rather than being isolated in our pairs. The stoves purred away, melting snow to water, as we wrapped ourselves in down jackets and drank tea. Once more, I suggested it would be cool just to stop and have a day off, but my idea got short shrift from the others so I let it go. And when we got out the food supplies to have a proper look we realised that there was very little left indeed. That night we took only half a meal each. Cathy and I shared our first and only freeze-dried meal of the trip and drank more tea.

The team was divided over tactics. Zarok, Rangdu, Nuru and Cathy, as well as Rick, were all pushing to go for the summit next day, while I was still thinking we should rest up, perhaps move our camp higher so as to cut a few hundred metres from our summit day. We still had almost a thousand metres of ascent to go. The others were adamant. Given the lack of food, the Sherpas said that in their opinion we had to go for the summit tomorrow or we would starve. Rick was pushing a bit too, and given that I didn't mind that much, the decision was made. I knew better than to waste energy by trying to convince them otherwise.

As the day wore on the wind got up; the weather forecast had predicted winds of thirty miles per hour and that concerned me. Even at 4,000 metres that would be close to borderline for a summit attempt. At 8,000 metres it felt to me completely unrealistic. I expected the others to review the plan, but they had their minds set and that was that. I felt detached, as though I was observing us all from another perspective – outside myself looking down.

The lack of food was driving the others on but I wasn't too worried; supplies were low, but we were getting on okay. I had known we would have very few supplies left by this stage and so felt mentally prepared for the situation. It didn't seem that important in the grand scheme of things. I was slightly concerned that we had run out of quick soups and powder drinks and sugar to add to water; at altitude they are a great way of getting energy. But as long as I knew we had some gas cartridges to melt snow I was happy enough. And if we had the luxury of something to add flavour to the meltwater, even an old teabag, then so much the better. Hydration was the main issue. We had enough body fat and muscle to burn for a day or two. When I got home the weight loss would benefit my rock climbing. But no water? That was a crisis.

I felt a bit outnumbered. The Sherpas were concerned and I understood their point of view. I could see they were tired. Cathy was too. Rick and I had done this sort of stuff before, although not for quite so long, and we knew that at this altitude one could hardly digest food anyway. But given that the team were so keen to keep moving, it would have been a brave leader to talk them out of their attempt. I worried about the wind; I wondered, given how tired the Lhakpas were, that they wouldn't want to try for the summit if it blew hard. I thought it would be the Sherpas who would be the stronger members of our team at this point. I fully expected us Westerners to be wasted by this stage.

All things considered, I decided it was best just to go with the flow and accept the democratic view. We discussed a plan and agreed to go to bed as soon as possible, wake at 11 p.m. and try to set off around midnight. We didn't really discuss the descent. That would be for the following day. It was generally assumed that if we did summit then the obvious descent would be by the Schell route, as we were camped right on it. With some good luck it would take about two days to descend back to the isolated herder village of Latabo. We finished our drinks and settled down for the night, having made sure our equipment was ready for the off in the wee small hours.

I dozed intermittently, but at 11 p.m. the tent fabric was flapping like crazy in the strong winds so we delayed things a bit, hoping the wind would ease. By 1 a.m. we were all ready. I was happy to give it a go but not wildly convinced we could get far in such strong winds; if one of the others had given me an indication of support for my wish to stay put I would have readily called a halt. I felt like crap, and the thought of a first ascent was way down my list of motivational incentives. The wind was too strong and I knew it. I struggled to walk and adjust my head torch, goggles and various hoods all at the same time.

At first I was right at the back as the others climbed off into the night. I was roped to Rick, who was at least semi-patient. He knows that under stress I can vomit most of my breakfast and then feel fine and start functioning as well as anyone. He slowed the pace slightly for me and we managed to keep up with the others. The route we were taking was steep as we tried to follow the natural line along the main crest of the ridge. Rock features curved steeply upward, dividing the Rupal and Diamir faces. The climbing was superb, quite hard at times but never too technical. There were a few occasions when we had to stop and climb one at a time, but in general we all moved together, making good progress.

The wind-chill persuaded us to keep moving; we needed the heat of exercise in the black night. As light slowly crept in from the east, the view around us deepened and took shape. I became aware of the huge exposure below me and to the right where the Rupal Face plunged into the shadows. At around 6 a.m., after climbing for five hours, we came to a little summit from where I expected the ridge to continue in a relatively straightforward line to the Merkl Notch at around 7,900 metres. It was here that Reinhold Messner and his brother Günther had endured the bitter cold of their bivouac after reaching the summit in 1970.

Now we discovered that the terrain was more complicated, exposed and technical than any of us had expected. Seeing the terrain ahead of us, with the summit so far away, Nuru and Cathy became totally despondent. Perhaps they thought the summit we were on would have been much closer to the true summit; as it turned out there were other similar intermediate summits to overcome before we got to the top. They both seemed physically tired and emotionally worn out. Cathy told us she wanted to turn back. Since Nuru had agreed to team up with Cathy if she opted to descend, he untied from Zarok and swapped ropes with Rangdu, who had been climbing with Cathy.

It was a sad moment, but a realistic decision. Encouraging words from the rest of us would have made no difference. We decided to descend slightly as this seemed an easier line to the summit, but climbing down proved very awkward and much more technical than I thought it would, and more time-consuming. At times we'd have to torque our ice axes into cracks, or hook them over spikes and lower ourselves down steep overhanging walls while the wind blew updrafts of loose snow into our faces. We balanced our crampons on tiny ledges in the rock. The climbing was all determined and rather ungraceful. In a few places it was easier just to let ourselves drop.

After descending like this for a couple of hundred metres, we came to a place where it seemed that Cathy and Nuru could traverse back on easier snow ramps, with relative ease, to our bivvy at 7,160 metres. We, aiming for the summit, would be faced with a very steep wall leading to a small snow band with the summit pyramid beyond. We said our goodbyes, but didn't take long about it. Time was pressing and the wind was as strong as ever. 'Take care then, mind how you go,' I said. 'Catch you later.' And then we were off in opposite directions.

The climbing was technical, Scottish III or IV, with much loose rock. It was pointless putting in protection since the wall was so friable and loose. Anyway, Zarok and Rangdu had our few pitons and nuts with them. Rick and I were happy moving together on this type of terrain. I tried where possible to flick the rope over spikes and that offered some sense of security, but we knew that falling off was not an option. Soloing on this kind of ground is a necessary part of climbing new Himalayan routes in alpine style. The climbing was absorbing and the absolute focus required seemed to relax my mind. I thought of little else but the moves in front of me. Time flowed past; I focused on my breathing, filling my lungs, keeping the rhythm. I controlled my mind, kept it tight on a leash, so that I didn't raise my expectations that the worst was over. I needed to keep within my limits so we could keep going for hour after hour. There would be more ahead, the altitude would be higher, and the air thinner. I needed to accept that.

Rangdu was in front and Zarok followed on the other end of their rope, taking a curving line up the face. I saw how much slack they had between them and insisted that Rick and I stop to coil our rope, putting the spare into the top of my sack. Now with twenty-five metres of rope between myself and Rick, I followed the approximate line Rangdu had taken, but a little more directly to avoid any stones they might accidentally send down. There was some soft snow, but the wind had blown much of it from the steep rock and, as a consequence, our route diverged some more as we followed a route parallel to that of the Sherpas.

I was enjoying myself, overcoming this obstacle with my good pal on the other end of the rope, but was concerned that we still had a long way to go. I was also kicking myself that we hadn't researched this upper section of Nanga Parbat more thoroughly. We'd been thinking so hard about the Mazeno that we rather thought the rest would take care of itself. Not many people had been this way: the Messner brothers, of course, on their famous descent from the Rupal Face; Hans Schell's team in 1976; and a handful of Spanish, Polish and Czech climbers. The problem was that I don't speak much German and the other languages even less, so I had hardly read any of their reports. I had scanned some pictures of this part of the mountain, but had to admit that I didn't absorb all the detail.

Back then I had been planning on taking the ridge between the Diamir and Rupal faces. I had assumed it would be technically difficult, but that we would cope with it. A climb that felt like a pipe dream had turned suddenly into reality – like being a teenager and knowing that you'll probably end up buying a house, but not caring too much about what kind of kitchen you want.

Despite the gaps in our knowledge, we were enjoying ourselves and closing in on 8,000 metres. We had reached easier ground and I now looked behind us to see how Cathy and Nuru were getting on traversing back to camp. I had thought the Sherpas might stop to have a drink once they reached the snow, but they were still bashing on. I felt a surge of frustration; they knew they should be looking after their bodies at this altitude. They weren't far ahead and I called out to them, but the wind was strong and there was no sign they had heard me.

Rick and I stopped for a quick drink from our water bottles and adjusted the rope so that we were now no more than twelve metres apart before moving off again. We were heading for a steep rock band above the Merkl Notch. As we reached it we met Rangdu and Zarok descending rather despondently toward us. I could see their footprints leading uphill and the point at which they had turned around. Why had they not waited for us? I felt a flash of anger that they'd made the decision for us. They seemed surprised that we were so close behind. Maybe they'd pushed on just to satisfy us that it really couldn't be done?

I scanned the steep wall ahead and, beyond that, the snow and rock slopes that led to the summit. There was still a long way to go, a good part of it above 8,000 metres. We stood together, the wind stinging our faces. The Lhakpas seemed really dejected. 'It's very steep up ahead and we are too late,' Rangdu said. It was now 11 a.m. or so. I looked up again, tracing a line past the wall and up systems of couloirs leading to the top. My friend Robert Schauer had been up there somewhere as part of Hans Schell's expedition. I knew I could climb it, but it was a long way. How long would it take us? My mind wound slowly through the calculations.

'We have to go, Mr Sandy,' Rangdu said. Zarok nodded in

agreement. Rick was silent. I thought, it's seven hours to the top if the climbing doesn't get much harder. We would get to the top at around five or six o'clock. I knew I was probably being optimistic. Then, of course, we would have to get down. We had head torches and perhaps half a litre of water each left in our bottles. Rick and I would probably have an open bivouac somewhere around the Merkl Notch. The Messners had done that, so it wasn't impossible. Then again, Günther had been in a ragged state and fallen to his death next day. And the Messner brothers were amazing.

The wind was now very strong, so if anything went wrong or my estimate was out we would get benighted and our bodies would be right on the limit – dehydrated, exhausted and exposed to the elements. I kicked myself: why did we not bring a stove? I sensed Rick running the same equations through his head. We have climbed together at these high altitudes for most of our lives. Our ambitions are often beyond what other people think is wise or possible, but we know our limits.

Rangdu was insistent. He is my friend too, I thought. With Zarok we have endured tough times together. It is too late and too windy. We don't really know how much climbing is left. I looked at them, deep into their eyes. I looked at Rick, who was, I assumed, as keen as me to keep going but also aware that without a stove or sleeping bags it was a risk too far. I wondered if he was also kicking himself?

'You're quite right, Rangdu,' I said. 'We have to go down. It's still early but we have been on the move since 1 a.m.'

'We want to go home,' Rangdu said. 'It's too much. There is no food left and it's too technical. We'll need a long time to climb this.' I'd been climbing long enough with Sherpas to know that once they've made their mind up, that's it. 'We are going down tomorrow,' he added. Really he was telling me that we all had to go down, that our attempts at the summit were over. It was obvious to me that both Rangdu and Zarok were done.

I looked at Rick, wondering what he would do. Like me,

he could happily cut loose and solo to the top. We'd done similar things before and I wondered if we were about to do it again. I felt as though I was in the middle of a game of mental chess. I felt calm and relaxed. In my notebook at home is a quotation from the industrialist Andrew Carnegie, born in Dunfermline: 'The man who acquires the ability to take full possession of his own mind may take possession of anything else to which he is justly entitled.'

I felt sympathy for Zarok and Rangdu but sensed also that Rick and I were keen to climb. I tried to take emotion out of it. I wanted to make sure that these two friends got back to camp. Their contribution to the expedition had been immense. They had been the key that unlocked this upper section to us. We had done what we had set out to do, and reached the Mazeno Gap with energy and supplies to spare and we'd done it as a team. I was aware that the wrong words from me now could unravel this strong team spirit. We had successfully traversed the Mazeno Ridge. Was that not enough?

I knew I had the strength to keep going, but the wind was too strong and we did not have a stove. Okay, I told myself, today is not the day.

'Right. Let's go down.'

Rangdu said, 'We are finished Sandy, down tomorrow!' Then he and Zarok turned and walked away. Rick and I took another look at the wall above and then turned after them, following the tracks back the way we had come. Within seconds I knew I had made the correct decision; I felt certain it was the correct call. Rick was with me.

After a few hundred metres I shouted to the Sherpas against the roar of the wind to stop. They waited and we grouped together. I explained I had seen a traverse ledge that cut the corner we'd made after we left Cathy and Nuru. It may be possible to descend more quickly and maybe come back up it next time. I noticed Zarok and Rangdu both ignored my comment about another attempt. But they were happy to descend another way if it saved time. Abandoning our tracks, we all walked directly down the slope. It was much easier walking straight downhill as the snow became shallower, but we had to take care not to trip on the loose rock beneath and fall down the cliff we were traversing above. Disappointment and exhaustion were creeping over us.

Despite this, the sun was shining and the wind had dropped now that we were in the lee of the summit slopes. We stopped for a drink and bite to eat, and I opened my zips to cool down a little. Then came an awkward traverse along a rock bench and I tore the front of my down trousers, inhaling a mouthful of expensive duck feathers which almost choked me. I continued down, placing my pick on the rock and easing my weight precariously down with the Sherpas following, grumbling about my route.

We came to some old fixed hawser rope, blanched white by the sun and degraded by exposure to the elements. Some big old pitons swung freely on a steep wall, high above us out of reach. The snow must have been deeper when the climbers who left them came through. They had secured fixed ropes, a line of safety back to base camp. We didn't have that luxury.

The traverse was tedious and scary, protection was minimal, so we occasionally hitched the rope over a spike. If one of us fell, our rope-mate would probably get pulled off too. Then we were past the traverse's difficulties and heading towards a snow ramp, which we hoped would lead easily to a rock buttress. Below this, easy climbing and a few abseils should take us back to camp. Cathy and Nuru should be there by now. I hoped they had the energy to melt some snow for us.

We were now quite exhausted, but by 2.30 p.m. had almost managed to traverse off the steep section. Two awkward abseils had brought us to an easy snow traverse that led to the ramp. The ground was steep and the snow softer. Now was the moment Zarok tripped on his crampon and fell. He tried to get his ice axe in to stop himself, but to no avail. I watched Rangdu kick himself into the soft snow, trying to get a good, solid stance in preparation for the rope going tight. Once again there was too much slack rope so the impact was high; as soon as Zarok's weight came on the rope, Rangdu was catapulted off his feet and fell after Zarok, passing him in a matter of seconds.

All Rick and I could do was watch helplessly. The two Sherpas continued to fall past each other; as one recovered the other would shoot past and drag him off his feet and down the slope again. I really thought they were going to go all the way down the Diamir Face. Then, by chance, just as they approached the edge of a band of ice cliffs, their direction of fall took them to a point where a huge sérac had lifted slightly. This change in angle was just enough to bring them to a halt, right on the edge of the cliff. I could hardly believe their good luck. They had stopped.

After a small delay both stood up, apparently uninjured. I waved and shouted but I am sure they heard nothing, my voice carried away in the light wind. Rick and I wanted to help, but it was obvious the two Lhakpas were well enough to extricate themselves. Rangdu was looking up at me. I wondered what he was thinking. Although they'd survived a terrifying fall, and were mentally celebrating a narrow escape, they had probably just realised that they now had the hard work of breaking a new trail back to the top of the ramp.

I made some hand signals to Rangdu, telling him that we would traverse downwards to come closer to them. If they took an easy rising traverse we would meet them halfway and could continue breaking trail more directly to the upper reaches of the snow ramp. Then it would be a short climb down to camp. We seemed to understand each other and I watched them untangle their rope and move upwards on a low-angled rising traverse. I set off with Rick and it was easier now we were traversing downhill. Soon we were reunited with Zarok and Rangdu.

The four of us sat and chatted, Rick and I consoling the Sherpas. They were shattered, blown away by their near-miss. It had been incredibly good luck to come to a halt where they did. Zarok and Rangdu had clearly had enough of Nanga Parbat and spoke emotionally about their experience. There was no way they'd be coming back for another go. We encouraged them to keep moving and get back to the tents, sharing the dregs of our water with them before continuing uphill, desperate work in the softening snow.

As we slogged up to the snow ramp, we found an old stash of supplies, which Rick was enthusiastic to explore. The tins were labelled in German. I simply ignored it, knowing that while there was a slight chance some of the food might be of use, a good brew at camp would be much nicer. Rick found some dried fruit, offering it around as he ate some. I declined, not wanting to risk poisoning myself. While Rick dug through the tins and packets like a magpie, I whiled away the time looking at the view and reflecting on our situation. Rangdu and Zarok were desperate to get back to camp and quickly disappeared behind some steep rocks.

The view was spectacular. The Mazeno Ridge and all its 7,000-metre peaks were shrouded in a wonderful mist that reflected the dwindling sunlight. Rick and I had no need to talk but I am sure that we both understood we were approaching a crossroads in the expedition. It was simpler for Rick to occupy himself with burrowing through the decades-old stash than voice opinions. Besides, events were too fresh. I felt I needed time to let the dust settle. I looked behind me and traced the traverse line of our descent with my eyes. I was trying to etch it into my memory so that I could find it in a storm. It was a habit I had developed as a kid initially gathering sheep on the Haughs of Cromdale and then navigating my way on the featureless arctic plateau of my beloved Cairngorms.

The truth, as I saw it, was that Cathy and Nuru were despondent and knackered. I assumed they had made it back to camp, but there was as yet no sign of them. Rangdu and Zarok were most definitely at their wits' end. Was there any human who would not be, having gone through so much? Rick and I were dealing in our own ways with the range of emotions of a failed summit attempt and the sight of the two Sherpas sliding uncontrollably towards their deaths.

I needed quietness and time to think. I was happy to be alive, happy that all the team were alive. I also knew we should not have set out in the wind early that morning. We had burned up scarce resources which we could ill afford to lose. I should have been more confident in my own assessment of the situation. I should have found the courage to tell the others that leaving at 1 a.m. in that wind was silly. Then again, I realised that they would have simply tried without me. It's not called summit fever for nothing. Why had I fallen for such temptation?

Perhaps I should not have been so insistent about a new line to the summit – Rick and Cathy had always advocated taking the easier line to the summit if we did get through to the Mazeno Gap. I knew there was an easier snow couloir lower down that would be a good way to top out. Sitting on the rocks, waiting for Rick, I looked back at our descending steps and saw there was a potential line. It would lead us to the upper Kinshofer route. But by that time Rick had had enough of tinkering about in the abandoned food dump and was packing a corroded tin of something into his rucksack. I thought he was nuts but knew better than to comment.

'Come on,' I said, 'let's get out of this wind and have a cup of tea.' Down we went. I took a nice photo of the setting sun and the mist-wreathed Mazeno. As I took the double fisherman's knot out of one of my prusik loops and threaded the thin cord around a spike for the final abseil, I wondered if I would come back to this place again. Mentally I was preparing myself for our arrival at the tents. It would be ace to get a brew in my hand from Cathy or Nuru. But I felt that when we joined the others the mood would be bleak.

06

SPLITTING UP

The sun was setting and the light fading as Rick and I arrived at camp. Stoves were burning in two of the tents, while the tent I shared with Cathy was eerily quiet. Nuru was back and now sticking his head out of the door of his tent, obviously pleased to have his partner Zarok back. Cathy was half asleep inside our tent; she seemed okay but tired and disappointed. I was grateful to see she had a full pot of hot water for me.

I took my time coiling the ropes, which had been left in a jumble, and stashed them on a big stone by the tent. I slowly took off my crampons, wrapping the straps tidily around them and lacing them to the same rock. Then I went and spoke to both the other teams through the tent walls. Rick, Rangdu and Zarok did not show their faces; exhaustion ruled and it was clear that this was not a time for discussion. I imagined each of them in their sleeping bags, busy melting snow and rehydrating. I wished everyone a good night and went back to my own tent.

Cathy told me that she and Nuru had got back to camp around 9 a.m. and had been brewing all day. She told me they were all going down. I had very little to eat – there was little food left now, just drinks. Changing into my dry socks, I snuggled into my sleeping bag and wished Cathy good night. I said the Lord's Prayer in my mind and thought of Hannah and Cara back home. The expedition is over, I thought to myself. They are all for descending the Schell route tomorrow. I wondered if they realised how dangerous it was. I didn't know what I would do, but I felt our summit attempt had burned us up. Sleep came easily.

I woke next morning feeling refreshed. It was 13 July and it felt like we'd been on this mountain forever. After such a hard day yesterday I was pleasantly surprised to feel so good. Cathy was rustling around in her sleeping bag beside me and the stove was on and melting snow in the little pot. Rangdu's voice interrupted my thoughts and our tent got a rattling as he shook the overnight build-up of frost. I sensed that he was really making sure we were both awake.

'Sandy, it's time to go down. We are leaving soon!'

Sitting up in bed, I felt surprisingly buoyant and relaxed, even positive – the kind of positivity I often wake up with back home in my comfortable bed at sea level. It's the kind of wide-awake alertness that can be incredibly annoying to others who take longer to come around in the morning.

Was it too late? The others were obviously still resolute in their decision to go down and the Sherpas were keen to make a start as soon as possible. The cumulative effect of so much time at altitude had made them assume that since we hadn't reached the summit yesterday we should now abandon our climb. There had been a dramatic shift of balance. The team seemed to be unravelling, unable to consider other alternatives. Their need to rush disturbed my calm mood; why couldn't they just be at peace?

Yesterday's summit bid had been arduous and the Sherpas' fall dramatic. It's normal to be exhausted after a summit bid on an 8,000-metre peak and a natural instinct to get swept up in the idea that you have to descend. The fact that I was feeling so good was exceptional and caught me off guard. I wanted to take the time to chat, to shoot the breeze and drink tea, to reflect on where we were. I did not want to get up or rush around. I did not want them heading down just because of one failed attempt.

The Lhakpas were already busy striking tents, packing their equipment ready to descend to the safety of Latabo Camp and then on to Tarshing and a lift to the Shangrila in Chilas. I supposed they had in their minds the oasis of a big hotel room with warm showers, wide beds and well-prepared meals. Me, I was not thinking in these terms at all. I was in no hurry to go anywhere. I knew the summit was there for the taking and I felt I had the energy to try again. In my youth I had soloed some quite big winter climbs in the Alps but I didn't wish to do the same on this incredible summit. Still, it was worth considering. At the very least, I wanted to have the time to consider my options. I needed to think about this.

I wondered if the others realised they were pressurising themselves – as well as me – with all their rushing around. I understood they were exhausted. I thought perhaps that after spending all these days traversing the ridge and sleeping so high, they would be superbly acclimatised. Could they not see that if they could get past this state of mind and relax and rehydrate they might feel differently? I felt certain we could make some sort of recovery even at this altitude – but we had to take a rest day and let that happen. I hoped that time might help them adjust to the disappointment of our abortive summit attempt.

I wondered why I had a different set of priorities inside my head. I saw no real hurry to rush a decision. The descent had been there for years; it wasn't going anywhere. And it was far from an easy option. I understood it might be safer to descend the big snow slopes before the sun reached its zenith. But the snow was unconsolidated anyway. To me it seemed too emotional, this rush to strike the tents and pack up. I hoped to encourage the others to slow down, like holding my crying daughters when they got themselves worked up, holding them in my arms against my chest, breathing deep, hoping that my peace and the security of being held against their father's body would calm them.

Again, I heard Rangdu's voice: 'Come on Sandy, we have to go soon.' I'm not sure what really happened next. I do remember calling out: 'Hey Rick, do you want to come over here and discuss our options.' He called back to me that he would and soon appeared at the tent dressed and ready to chat. He looked serious but relaxed, a little tired perhaps but then I suppose we all were.

When I saw him, I wondered if my own thoughts were realistic or whether I was being influenced by the desire to summit at all costs. Was my ego just trying to hang on to an eighteen-year-old ambition to complete this unclimbed ridge? Maybe I was the one with the deranged thoughts.

Rick was himself: skinny and a bit grey, my reliable buddy, especially at extreme altitude. I told him I didn't want to rush, that I would like to take my time and stay for a while, and that I had no idea what I planned to do, but that I saw no need to rush down. 'Let's simply take the day off and rest up,' I suggested. He agreed, with the briefest of camouflaged smiles. He knows me so well, I thought, and I felt reassured that I was being sensible, that I was not trying to achieve an impossible dream.

Cathy got up out of her sleeping bag and packed up her gear. She seemed to share the Sherpas' sense of urgency, wanting to keep moving and start down. I suggested we stayed, but none of them liked that idea at all. Cathy finished packing; Nuru and Zarok had their tent down and rolled up and were starting to pull the pegs and boulders from our tent. I asked them to slow it down. They were adamant that they were going to go down. I sat at the unzipped door of my tent and said: 'Hey Rangdu, come here for a chat.'

He came closer, seemingly exhausted, his face swollen with altitude. He seemed worse than Rick looked and I felt. The Sherpas had worked harder than any of us. I could see that their fall yesterday had scared them and Rangdu showed the emotion of that today. He is a tough man, I thought. Rangdu was no high-altitude virgin. I explained that while I knew we had suggested yesterday that we should go down, now I felt strong after a good night's sleep. I thought they should not rush and we could maybe do a bit more.

He told me he had made up his mind. We should all go down. I was in the doorway of my tent, sitting on my sleeping bag. My bare feet stuck out of the door while I pulled on my socks. I said again that I would really like it if he would consider staying up here with Rick and me. 'I know Cathy, Nuru and Zarok definitely want to go down. Are you willing to stay?'

He looked at me. 'No.' He said it nicely but he meant it. He turned to Nuru and Zarok, spoke long sentences in Sherpa, some of which I semi-understood. I assumed he wished to make it really clear to the other Sherpas what I was saying, but the three men were all in agreement. They would go down. I said I was sorry. He said in his broken English: 'I am very tired. Very hard yesterday. There is no food left. We will die if we stay here. Too much danger.' He was adamant that we should all descend together.

All mountain guides are used to clients saying that they want to turn back. With experience you understand when it's appropriate to encourage them to go on and when it's obvious that they've had enough. It's a really fine judgement but over the years I think I've become reasonably good at making it. So often, when I've persuaded someone to keep going, they've reached the summit and been gloriously happy. Back in the valley they've thanked me for pushing them. They say things like: 'There was no way I thought I could do that!' It's a truly rewarding feeling to see people achieve things beyond their imagination. Humans can far exceed their own expectations most of the time. The situation here, at 7,160 metres on Nanga Parbat, was not the place to encourage people to keep going. These four wonderful climbing partners had truly had enough. They knew they were sailing in dangerous waters and that they must escape soon. The summit was no longer an option.

Cathy wrote afterwards in her blog that she thought Rick and I were crazy with summit fever. (I did ask her to help write this account but she declined: 'The only time I agreed to write a book with someone else I had to do all the work, so no thanks.') She thought at the time that Rick and I were stepping across the line from acceptable risk to something altogether more dangerous.

At that point, I don't think either Rick or I had a plan. We just wanted to rest, hang out for the day and then make the decision.

The conversation had been matter-of-fact but not hostile. There was no resentment. But for me, sadly, the utopia of our collective solidarity was over. The team was splitting. Cathy, Rangdu, Zarok and Nuru would leave as soon as they were ready.

We did not allocate things; to all intents and purposes all our food had been eaten anyway. The others helped themselves to what they thought they needed and what was reasonable to take, but there were only leftovers. Rick and I would keep one tent, a rope and a stove so that we could be our independent selves. We had both been here before. A couple of days without food were acceptable so there was no point in discussing it; it was pointless burning mental energy on something we couldn't change. There were lots of gas cylinders left so there was no need to think too carefully – our most fundamental requirement, to stay hydrated, could be met.

By now we were all dressed and had our boots on. Rick seemed tired but pleased we did not have to rush down. We both helped organise things. Cathy took her gear out of our tent and Rick moved in. Soon all was tidy. I took the phone from Cathy and she explained how it worked. She had been using it to receive weather forecasts and update our social media. Occasionally we'd had a message back; it was great for us all to know our families and friends back home were getting good news about us. About three-quarters of the battery power remained and we felt confident that was enough. There was a second satellite phone with Samandar at Base Camp. It was likely he would have struck our base camp at the foot of the Mazeno and moved everything down to Latabo, the herder's camp at the foot of the Schell route by now.

Although we hadn't discussed the plan in fine detail, I had every confidence in Samandar and his team. The broad outlines of the expedition had been sorted out long before we arrived in Pakistan. They knew what to do and there was no need at this stage for me to get tangled up in arrangements in the valley. My dad taught me years ago that it was pointless to buy a guard dog and then start barking yourself. Rick, Cathy and I debated whether we even needed the phone. I really don't like carrying phones or radios. When I was younger we had no such communication devices and life was simple and grand and we got by well enough. While I see and do appreciate the many advantages of phones and radios, they are reliant on battery power and these batteries can be incredibly unreliable in the intense cold of high altitude. And the heavy apparatus and the battery itself weigh almost the same whether they are empty or full. When one has to carry everything on one's back, devices with flat batteries are useless items that you can't eat.

Communications can also bring news that can really affect the spirit of a team. I remember feeling robbed when I guided Everest for the first time after I came down from the summit with my client and went to phone my mother. It was a delight to hear her voice on the phone and I said I was calling to say hello and tell her that we had made it to the top and were safely back at camp. 'Oh,' she said, 'I heard that several days ago. It's all over the internet.' How could other people steal my life from me like that? Of course, none of this has stopped me having the latest iPhone.

There seemed to be three reasons we might want to make a call. First, to let the others know our general plan, whether we were descending or not. Second, we might want to let them know we'd reached the summit and, third, tell them our descent route so they could send lighter shoes and clothing and a jeep to the roadhead. Three-quarters of a battery should be sufficient for that as long as we kept the calls short and treated the batteries with respect by keeping the phone as warm as possible.

Cathy also gave me a 'spot meter', essentially a personal locator device. Through my work with the Scottish Avalanche Information Service back at home I had already gained some experience of something similar. She said it would transmit the user's coordinates and their progress could then be tracked on a computer. I could not really imagine why I should carry it and why I would want to go home and spend even more of my time on a computer to see where I knew I had already been. Again I thought I would have preferred to carry the equivalent weight in chocolate or scones, jam and cream. But she was quite insistent. I suppose it would tell people where our dead bodies were located. She also reassured me I needn't touch it at all: it was all set up to continue doing its thing. I tossed it into my sack and totally forgot about it.

It wasn't long before our descent team were packed up and ready to go. I tried to explain to the Sherpas where the Schell route went and remind them of what I'd pointed out when we camped at Latabo. I was worried for them. The Mazeno Ridge is quite inescapable, so the Schell route is the first easier-angled topographical feature available from the Mazeno Gap and that was the only reason it was chosen. It was far from safe and straightforward. Most people who had tried the Schell since its first ascent in 1976 had suffered accidents on it. We had first-hand knowledge of this from Doug Scott. In 1992, during one of his attempts on the Mazeno, his team had suffered some horrendous rockfall and Valeri Pershin had been badly hurt. Doug told me that most people would have gone home to hospital after such a bad accident, but the Russian just stayed at Base Camp and waited for his injuries to heal. On top of that, no one had tried to climb it for years, so there would be no tracks, old fixed ropes or man-made landmarks to follow.

So although we had always thought of the Schell as one of our planned descent routes, we all knew it was a very serious climb and that to descend it in these snow conditions was very committing. I warned Rangdu that they had to be incredibly careful of the snow. As expedition leader I was letting two-thirds of our team descend without their leader; as a mountain guide I felt incredibly responsible for them. This wasn't a professional situation and I was not legally burdened with the responsibilities associated with working with clients as a mountain guide, but I was worried. Would we ever see them again? What if they got avalanched, or experienced rockfall? Would they find the way? If they went missing, what would the climbing world think of me as a leader? How would I live the rest of my life? How might such guilt mentally affect me?

The world had been quick to judge Reinhold Messner after he lost his brother Günther when descending from the first ascent of the Rupal Face. It seemed that we had been following almost in their footsteps, pushing a hard route on Nanga Parbat. Would I face the same criticism as Reinhold? I would hate to be in Reinhold's shoes, to have people continually wondering what really had happened up there.

It's hard for climbers to understand what happens on a large and complex expedition on such a big peak, let alone the general public or a court of law. And the 1970 expedition did end up in court, with Reinhold and the expedition's leader Herrligkoffer suing and counter-suing each other over a number of years. Conditions are wild on 8,000-metre peaks. Climbing them without oxygen and surviving unplanned bivouacs takes its toll. Hypoxia and exhaustion mess with your mind – with your decision-making as well as your memory of those decisions. People who have not climbed in such conditions and experienced what it is truly like to be pushing the limits of what is humanly possible can't fully understand.

Those writing books about other people's efforts sometimes over-analyse or criticise a climber's choices in extreme circumstances. I sometimes wonder how writers even begin to understand what it is like. I have spent enjoyable periods of time with mountaineering historians and they are always kind and seem very nice. I remember being in a supermarket with one very nice fellow as he tried to choose a bottle of wine. It took him ages. Making decisions in retrospect in the comfort of one's own study is an easier proposition than the decision an exhausted high-altitude climber has to make spontaneously, high on a mountain.

Imagine for a moment how dreadful it must have been for Reinhold Messner to experience his sibling falling to his death. As an older brother it must have been desperate. They had just made the first ascent of what is considered to be the highest vertical drop in the world. Making fine moral distinctions when your brain is failing isn't easy.

Still, German, Austrian and Tyrolean climbers spent years pursuing each other through the courts after Hermann Buhl's amazing first ascent and after Messner's ascent of the Rupal. The arguments were bitter and personal. It's sometimes said that each member of a team goes on their own expedition which is distinct from that of their teammates. Rick, Cathy, the three Lhakpas and I had no official contract among us, about climbing or writing, or the use of each other's photographs. We simply went climbing and trusted each other to be respectful, honest and kind.

There were no complaints when the team split, and no criticism when Rick and I decided to stay. I was reassured by the respect I had for the skill and experience of Cathy and the three Lhakpas; they were all experienced mountaineers and had made their own choices. We had been together on this mountain for a long time and had endured eleven nights at altitude. In the last few days we'd been reduced to the barest rations and, in this wilting state, their desire to descend was urgent. They must have felt within themselves that they were almost out of energy and had to go before it was all gone.

I was semi-confident they would do the right thing, and I hoped they had the energy and self-discipline to hold it together and make sensible decisions. I was also well aware that once they had committed to the descent, even if they ran into the most horrible and dangerous snow conditions, they would be hard pressed to find the energy to come back up. Anyway, there would have been little point in climbing back up to the Mazeno Gap to descend the Diamir Face. That would have been an even riskier proposition. Their options were few; we had got ourselves into that position and, having abandoned their summit hopes, their choice was simple. They had to go down. None of this was unforeseen, but now it was happening, it felt momentous.

We said our goodbyes, and hugged briefly. I think they were wondering about us, what the two of us were up to, staying where we were. I felt an extraordinary compassion and empathy as I leaned against a big boulder and watched them go, in two ropes of two, Cathy with Rangdu, behind Zarok and Nuru who were blasting a trail downhill. There was a light mist and the four figures became blurred and indistinct and then were gone.

We said nothing. Rick and I simply watched until our friends had disappeared into the grey mist. I felt very subdued but also calm. In my head I was humming Spirit of God, Unseen as the Wind, a traditional Scottish hymn set to the music of the Skye Boat Song. As a kid I had gone to church and to Sunday school. My mother was a Free Presbyterian and, with my twin brother Greg and sister Eunice, I had to endure Sundays indoors. Often we'd go to church more than once on the same Sunday. Despite the years of wild living, taking acid in the Alps and climbing with Mark Miller, the spiritual life never left me. Friends from the old days find it hard to understand that underneath it all I have a deep spiritual commitment, that I go to church, and say my prayers under my breath several times throughout the day.

I don't know whether this is the result of a Calvinist upbringing or an outstandingly charmed life, but I have a strong sense of being guided and cared for. I remember working on a training course in Rio de Janeiro, assessing rope-access technicians. I was overworked and jetlagged, and decided to delay my flight in order to take a day to catch up. Early next morning I went to the training centre to catch up on paperwork before the next batch of technicians arrived. As I sat focused on the keyboard of my laptop, the secretary who had been organising everything for me came in and put her hand on my shoulder.

'Hey, Sandy, you are the luckiest man in the world.' I looked up, surprised. 'That Air France flight you were supposed to be on this morning went missing with no survivors.'

The hairs on my neck stood on end and my whole body shivered. My heart went out to all the people on that aircraft, their families, relatives and friends. Why was I being so well looked after? I have many good reasons for my strong Christian faith – even though the pomp, ceremony and especially the long-winded prayers in my own Church of Scotland drive me nuts. Rick, I should say, is much more religiously disciplined than I am. But right then, sitting on that rock and watching Cathy and the three Lhakpas heading off down the west shoulder of Nanga Parbat, I felt at peace.

There was a brilliant light within me and that light stays with me and I hope never to lose it. I was thinking of how these ace team players had abandoned all hope of the summit. Their ambition to climb the mountain had died. I understood that a different set of priorities prevailed. They wished to retreat, while Rick and I had other plans. I had no concern at all for myself and Rick. I just knew, most certainly, that whatever we did, as long as we maintained our self-discipline, continued to play by the rules and maintained good, sensible decision-making, we would be fine. I felt strong and full of a spiritual grace.

I could not work out why I had had such a great night's sleep. Yes, I had been tired, but it was more than that. I felt reinvigorated psychologically. I just needed to have a day off and then I would make good decisions based on facts rather than emotion. I wondered if it was my decision or if I was being guided.

Yep, I thought, and wandered back to the tent. Rick put on some snow to melt and at that moment I realised my lighter was in Cathy's pocket, heading away from us down the Schell route.

Rick and I only had one lighter between us.

07

PUSHING ON

Rick and I sorted out our tent and made some drinks; then we went through the food. There wasn't much left but, as Doug Scott always said, 'it's better in than out, Sandy,' so we decided we should simply eat it and get our bodies ready for the next phase of the climb. With the others gone, Rick and I were left with the princely riches of about half a packet of digestive biscuits, and some scraps of peanut butter and crackers. We decided to keep the digestives for our summit attempt and consumed every other remaining scrap. It was still very little, not even the equivalent of one small meal between the two of us. At least we still had three or four gas cylinders. We would not run out of water.

We talked about going for a walk but when we started out we felt listless, so wandered to the beginning of the steeper ground, only a few hundred metres or so from the bivouac site, and agreed that we didn't need to bother. So we went back and sat around the tent, temporarily but contentedly directionless. At some point we got talking about what to do but I can't really remember much of that discussion. We knew that we were going to have another go at the summit. We didn't work this out; Rick and I just felt we could try again. It was twelve days since we'd left Base Camp. Morale had collapsed a little on the previous day, but now the negativity had lifted.

I was pleased to find that I'd got the amount of gas right during the planning stage. Running out of water isn't an option, not for long anyway. As for the food, people at lectures often ask me why we didn't carry more. The simple answer is that we carried as much as we could. There's a limit to these things. Anything more than eight or ten days' worth means you can't lift your rucksack. Alpine style is sometimes called lightweight style, but there's nothing light about it. For those who are critical of the approach, I can only recommend they try mixed climbing at 7,000 metres on a knife-edge ridge. It's hard enough to carry a sack with four or five days' food. But twice that?

Perched in our high camp, I was still a bit shocked that Lhakpa Rangdu was gone. He's among the strongest Sherpas I've ever met, and they're an amazingly strong bunch at altitude. The fact that Rick and I were still here was not a total surprise, but I'd hoped Rangdu would be with us. It had certainly been part of my plan and his absence was disconcerting. He is so strong and wise at altitude. All the Sherpas had made an incredible contribution. We would never be on this springboard without their effort. Trail-breaking along the ridge had been desperate at times and their efforts had been immense. Their role had been the crucial ingredient in our success.

Rick and I discussed when to wake up; we both felt that we shouldn't make a midnight start again. Climbing in the coldest and darkest hours is debilitating and we felt we needed to sleep and restore our bodies more. We also wanted daylight to help us surmount the steep rock section we had abseiled previously. It was obvious that we should not try the line I had insisted on for our first summit attempt. Considering our position, the lack of food and our general exhaustion, it would have been very audacious, not to say foolhardy. But traversing the Diamir flank seemed the easy option – too easy – even though it was the route Rick and Cathy had suggested from the outset. I still felt unhappy about it.

We decided that initially we would follow the line we had taken on our descent with Rangdu and Zarok the day before, and then see if we could traverse across to join the Kinshofer route. I could in my mind's eye calculate the distance involved and picture the undulating snow surface – the way it reflected the light indicating deep unconsolidated snow. I was not concerned about navigation but my brain ached at the idea of breaking trail at high altitude in such deep snow.

It would be soul-crushing work. I wished we were taking a steeper route; I simply hate walking and would much prefer to climb. Once again, I wished Rangdu were still with us to help. I hoped the weather would stay reasonably good, so that our tracks would not get covered; any kind of wind would fill them with drifting snow. I wondered at the amount of time we'd been up here; it's not something humans are made to do, live this long at altitude. We shouldn't really be here. Would slogging up those tracks again wring us out? Would it take the last of our life energy? Were we setting ourselves up for failure?

Rick and I had a final brew lying in our sleeping bags, and then I tucked my head into my hood and tried to sleep. Despite the anticipation of the next day's climb, the nerves and doubts, I felt at peace. I felt a wave of optimism. I imagined walking through the pine trees in Rothiemurchus near my home in the Cairngorms, sun filtering through the branches. I felt a spiritual energy that lifted me. I prayed that Cathy, the Sherpas, and my daughters and brothers and sister back home were safe and well. I was looking forward to getting back into the wild. It's where I feel at home. I was happy that with my pal Rick I was going to climb to the summit. Then, even though we'd be tired, we would drop down the Kinshofer route of the Diamir Face and join all the tourists climbing there. In no time at all we'd be at Base Camp.

Cocooned in my sleeping bag, I lay my head down to sleep. I felt secure; there was no point in worrying. We had stepped through a door into another world, one far beyond normality. Cathy may well think we are crazy old men, pushing too hard. But I knew it was where Rick and I expected to be at some point in our climbing lives. There had been other experiences, similar circumstances that had led us here. I had been in such places before.

I thought of Everest's north-east ridge, so high and remote, of turning my back on Doug Scott and Rick just below the pinnacles. The wind tore at us, icy crystals as sharp as sand blasting our outer clothing, spindrift filling my hood. I waved them good wishes as I went, a feral, inner voice telling me to go to ground, to escape the storm. At that point I thought Doug and Rick, my best friends, were crazy to even dream about continuing in those conditions. These were the pinnacles of the unclimbed Everest ridge, where Pete and Joe lay entombed, frozen in space and time. But a day later they came down to Advance Base Camp, exhausted but safe.

Now I felt we were experienced enough to be up here. I was confident that we had earned those stripes of endurance and determination. We had suffered before, and that suffering had fostered perseverance and resilience, what some people call character. Perhaps we really were climbing beyond ourselves, yet I felt brimful of hope, suffused with a quiet dignity. Of course there was a chance that we could die. That exists on all our days. But I was prepared, ready to climb above and beyond myself.

I wondered where these feelings came from. Are hope and love so different? These treasures we cannot see, measure or touch, save or accumulate? Yet, inexplicably, hope had accumulated in me. With this thought, without a care in the world, wrapped in grace and love for my family, friends and the mountains, I drifted easily into sleep. Tomorrow would take care of itself. Rick and I were on a road to somewhere special. There was no need to set an alarm.

When I woke, the tent was lined with frost and we carefully began the morning ritual of melting snow for tea. It was 14 July, an important day in my imagination, and not just for the storming of the Bastille in Paris in 1789. On the exact same day Sir Alexander Mackenzie, born in Stornoway on the Isle of Lewis, finally reached the mouth of the Canadian river that spills out into the Arctic Ocean and now bears his name. He had hoped it would bring him to the Pacific, but his dream of a north-west passage was broken. Several years later he did get there, carrying canoes, food and other equipment, with portages along turbulent rivers.

Men like Mackenzie have always inspired me. As a child, my mother supervised bedtime reading, handing me stories of explorers and Hudson Bay trappers that inspired my imagination. *White Fang* and *The Call of the Wild* were my favourite tales growing up. Here I was, in my fifties, still living those dreams, shoving my sleeping bag into my rucksack inside a frosty tent. We packed the stove and a gas cylinder and the remains of our food supplies, essentially the half packet of digestives. I remember that we paused to study each other's faces – checking our earlier decision not to take the bivouac tent and insulated sleeping mats. I would come to regret the absence of a mat.

Writing this now I don't really understand why we thought it, but at the time it seemed obvious to us that we would need just one long day to reach the summit, after which we would find traces of other climbers and join their well-trodden path, whizzing down fixed ropes to Base Camp laughing our heads off. The first time we had reached the summit, in July 2009, the winds were terrifying and we were glad to make it back to our high camp. The following day we had woken early and made a hasty exit before others were stirring; I had managed to shoot all the way down to Base Camp in a single day. Even though that effort left me exhausted, the experience showed me that we could get down the mountain quickly. We must therefore have felt that overloading our rucksacks with heavy bivouac equipment was a luxury we could do without at this stage. We would have one bivouac and be back in Base Camp late in the evening of 16 July.

Memory can sometimes prove a little fickle. In 2009 the route had indeed been fixed with ropes, but it was still quite serious. Serious enough, in fact, for Go Mi-Sun, a well-known Korean climber, to fall to her death and for another climber to be blown clean off the summit, never to be found. Our experience told us that we could get off Nanga Parbat in about a day and a half if the Diamir was fixed and the normal route well trodden by other climbers. Go Mi-Sun's death was a shocking reminder that it does not matter how many 8,000-metre peaks one climbs, each step you take has to be done with care and attention.

I wondered briefly how the Lhakpas and Cathy were getting on with their descent down the Rupal flank. (It turned out they had a tough time. They got avalanched and Cathy lost the memory card from her camera with all her images. Rangdu suffered a sprained ankle that turned out to be broken when it was X-rayed back in Kathmandu. But they still managed to reach Latabo the day after they left us.) Then I shouldered my pack, feeling quite confident for Rick and myself. If we failed to reach the top, we could keep traversing and descend the Diamir Face by the Kinshofer route, which we knew, or return part way along the ridge and descend via the route Reinhold Messner soloed in 1978. I knew Luis Stitzinger and Josef Lunger had descended Messner's route through the steep and jumbled séracs of the Diamir flank. It looked like suicide on first inspection, but if luck was on your side, you were moving fast and none of the séracs moved, it could be safe enough. Those three climbers had got down without incident so perhaps it was not such a game of Russian roulette as I initially suspected. It was at least another potential exit strategy. To be forced by circumstance to retreat back to this camp would have been difficult; the thought of following our own team's descent line down the Schell route was not an option. We didn't consider it. In fact, to be quite honest, descending to escape was not an option we considered seriously, although I only understood that in retrospect. Maybe us mountaineers do analyse all our options, if only subconsciously.

The critical thing was to get down as fast as we could. That's pretty much obligatory for those reaching the summit of an 8,000-metre peak without oxygen. It's nice to linger, to take some photos and absorb the intense fulfilment I usually feel. But at altitude, our bodies need just as much oxygen as normal, and at 8,000 metres the air pressure is a third of that at sea level. There's less oxygen available and we are constantly gasping for breath, like patients in intensive care, fighting for life, our blood saturation at critical levels. Even with my high-altitude discipline of taking time to fully inhale and fill my lungs with the greatest volume of air possible, I can only just breathe enough to keep standing still. My blood was thickening as we gained altitude, risking stroke and heart attack. Above 8,000 metres, even if you have access to abundant fluids, the body is dying fast. You have a few days at most up there.

The lack of oxygen also has a detrimental effect on mental processes. Rick and I had been climbing at high altitudes for two weeks now; our food intake had been scanty and it was just a matter of time before our bodies simply refused to do more and we would become incapable of movement. We were running out of time.

Still, packing our sacks, we were very sure that if we had indeed been the ones chosen to stay at this camp, it was surely ordained that we must get to the summit. I felt strong and confident and had no doubts that what we were doing was still reasonable. Our patience was paying off and pushing the boundaries of endurance seemed very possible.

It never occurred to us that once we reached the summit, finishing off our route, the descent would present anything more than the usual hurdles one can expect from a descent. We had not imagined we would have to struggle for our lives. I was just thinking positively. I even had the half-formed idea we could do an even bigger traverse and descend by Hermann Buhl's 1953 route. It wasn't remotely realistic with just half a packet of digestive biscuits, but I felt ebullient and full of confidence.

With a unity of purpose we zipped up the tent door and started our climb; it was around 8.30 a.m. Rick went first initially and we regularly swapped leads. The rope was properly adjusted with maybe twenty metres between us; the rest either wrapped around our shoulders in coils or packed away in the rucksack. The trail of our retreat from the first summit attempt had all but disappeared, covered by wind-blown snow. It was not going to be an easy traverse. We came to the old food cache Rick had rummaged through, and then we went on, ploughing up the deep snow. We tackled the rocky traverse that had so nearly led to disaster. It was technically much easier in ascent, and the step where I fell and tore my down trousers seemed quite easy. I looked down at the sticking plasters holding my trousers together.

We now had to leave the familiar route and take a rising line to a blind summit where we hoped we would pass an apparently insurmountable rock wall. This is always the best part of a new climb – the anticipation of new ground. Discovering and climbing the unknown gave me an incentive to keep moving forward through the desperate struggle for breath. Fortunately, the line we took brought us neatly below the steep cliff and with relative ease we moved up a snow ramp. This led to a small rock rib, which was quite blank and free of cracks. With careful placement of crampon points I led out over to its crest and an arête from where I could belay Rick safely.

Down the other side we went, a little awkwardly and not wanting to fall or slip. At the foot of the rib we were back on an easy snow slope, which meant we had to break trail again. We'd already had enough of slogging and became a bit despondent; walking for both of us is just a necessary evil to reach the bottom of a climb. Yet there was no getting around it. We had to grind on, slumping frequently over our ice axes, exhausted from the effort, hauling in each breath, resentful of the repetition and tedium. I tried to encourage myself with the thought that no one had been here before.

Up ahead we saw some couloirs which could offer climbing and excitement. Swapping leads, each of us taking turns out in front for several hundred metres at a time, we traversed around some small séracs and then climbed steeply up. I had the notion that this was the way Reinhold Messner had taken on his solo 1978 ascent but I didn't know for sure; there were varying reports about the route he had taken. A few snow showers pushed across; it was like traversing from the Arête du Midi above Chamonix round to the Cosmiques hut in bad weather – only with a fraction of the oxygen.

Large snowflakes fell heavily and stuck to our clothing, freezing any exposed skin. I became terribly cold and we had to pay close attention to our route finding. We huddled together at the top of the first steep section, discussing the concern that if this bad weather continued there would be no chance of continuing. We adjusted our clothing and decided it would be best to get away from this steep couloir; the snow seemed to be building fast and could start avalanching at any time.

Rather anxiously I took over the lead from Rick and, with a new sense of urgency, swarmed up the couloir until the rope stretched out and we continued together, hidden from one another by the falling snow. Then the snow stopped as suddenly as it had begun and we were once again climbing under blue skies. I felt my body relax as the snowfall diminished. Letting out some coils of rope from around my shoulders, I re-tied them securely at my waist and suggested that Rick kick himself a comfortable stance in the snow while I climbed up further. Eventually pulling over the top of an overhanging cornice, I felt a rush of gratitude as the pick of my axe sank securely into the hard-packed snow above. I was acutely aware that my flailing feet could dislodge snow debris large enough to knock Rick off his feet. It was exhausting work. With my lungs burning, I struggled on slowly, trying to control my frantic gasping for air.

Surmounting this couloir bought us close to the Diamir Face. I scanned the line of the Kinshofer route for activity – tents, climbers, anything that signalled human activity – but to my shock and amazement I realised the mountain was deserted.

There was no life at all. I had absolutely expected to see climbers on the face; they were always there at the height of the season. Not this year. I gazed across blank acres of rolling white snow, séracs, dark rocks and shattered ridges. There were no climbers at all, not so much as a half-filled boot print or an abandoned tent. I wondered why no one was climbing the normal route, but at the same time was rather pleased that we had the place to ourselves. Even so, the lack of other humans told me the Diamir Face must be plastered with deep snow and the avalanche potential must consequently be high; there was nothing else that could deter people from the climb.

We realised then that we were on our own. This was getting a bit more serious. Rick and I discussed it for mere seconds. We reasoned that the climbers were simply running late and perhaps had so far only reached the lower camps, which would be mostly out of sight to us. I actually thought we must have done well and were simply ahead of the game, getting so high so early in the climbing season. I decided that even with our acclimatisation and the long crawl along the Mazeno we had made such good progress that we might be ahead of the teams trying the normal route.

We had now been climbing solidly for thirteen days, whereas they would have been going up and down their route fixing ropes and camps. Giving myself a silent congratulatory pat on the back, I convinced myself that we must simply be ahead of the game. How could there be no one else on the mountain? The whole idea was preposterous. We dismissed it. We simply took pleasure in the idea that we had the upper mountain to ourselves and that the summit was still unvisited this year. It would simply be up to us to find the route to the summit.

The distance we had already covered was much further than expected, but the distance still to travel was immense. Now, of course, because we would be the first to the summit, we had to break trail and this section would take much longer than we had expected. We pushed on, taking turns to plough through the snow, until eventually I began to recognise some of the gargoyle-like boulders that decorate the upper part of the Kinshofer route. The terrain was not so steep, about thirty or forty degrees, but it was hard going in the snow.

Finally, at around 5 p.m., it became obvious that we were not going to reach the summit in daylight; the top was still many hours away. We debated whether we should keep going and try to find the summit in the dark, but better sense prevailed and we decided to use whatever daylight was left to make a snow cave. It was quite possible we would need shelter for a second night, especially if a storm came. So a plan began to hatch. We would dig a cave and make it a good one; it didn't matter how long it took. We could have a long lie-in tomorrow, get to the summit and then maybe return to the cave; our digging efforts wouldn't be wasted.

At the same time as we discussed what to do, I realised that spending two nights in a rudimentary shelter at such altitudes was a very risky business. I hoped dearly that we would dig the cave, have a great night's sleep, then get up early, reach the summit and descend to much lower altitudes. I was horribly aware that we were committing to even more time on the mountain, and at even higher altitudes. I'm used to dreaming of good food and green grass while high in the mountains. Now I was fantasising about thicker air nourishing my depleted body.

With the decision made, Rick led on for another section and then stopped at 7,720 metres to point out a good spot for digging. This was actually a daunting prospect: in our desire to sacrifice weight we hadn't brought our lightweight shovel. The thought of having to dig a snow cave with the tiny adzes of our ice axes was rather dismaying; it was like trying to empty a bath with a tea-spoon. I am an optimist though and it was a fine bank of snow. I felt certain it would be adequate for a snow shelter.

I suppose one could ask why we bothered digging in instead of just clearing a ledge and sleeping in the open. Rick and I are experienced snow-cave dwellers. We had used them on Pumori, when we had climbed a hard and technical new route on the steep unclimbed south face back in the 1980s. On that expedition we had lost our bivouac tent but, rather than abandon the climb, we simply dug long tubular snow-cave shelters – like coffins – behind the steep ice we were climbing and the rock beneath it. They were warm, out of the wind, and spindrift avalanches just passed over us while we were cocooned inside. We had also used snow caves high on Everest and of course at home in the arctic conditions of the Scottish Cairngorms in winter.

Rick and I made our rucksacks safe by carving a small shelf in the snow for them, adjusted our clothing so we wouldn't get too soaked with perspiration and set to work with the adzes of our ice tools. It was quite an intense effort and we had a sense of urgency as darkness fell and the temperature dropped further below zero. It was at least minus twenty-five degrees Celsius. We worked in silence, each in his own cave. It was quiet work, surrounded by the insulating snow. I found the quietness comforting, the cave itself womb-like. My pressing thought was to keep burrowing, to get it finished, lie down, get the stove on and start rehydrating. There was really nothing else to think about; we were animals, intent on survival. We wanted to be comfortable, to be able to lay flat in our sleeping bags. With proper shelter came security and the possibility of sleep – and recovery. Hopefully we would be in good condition to perform the following day.

Finally our two tiny tunnels broke through into one another and we both scraped away, enlarging the cave and pushing the last of the excavated snow between our legs and out of the entrance into the void beyond. Soon we had a good area where we were both able to lay full length. Sweeping out the last of the powder with our gloved hands, we sighed with relief. Now we could climb into our sleeping bags, light the stove and settle down to the chore of melting snow and quenching our never-ending thirst.

We drank tea and ate the remaining biscuits, and then positioned our rucksacks as pillows and closed off the opening.

I pulled my damp socks off and arranged them in my armpits to dry overnight while wearing my cleaner pair to sleep. I also pulled my wet gloves inside my sleeping bag, so that perhaps they might dry a little too. It was quiet and peaceful; we chatted a bit, mainly about how we had not realised it would still be so far to the top, and how we had not really anticipated a bivouac before we reached the summit, rather than after it, on the way down.

All we had to do the following day was reach the summit and then walk downhill. But we both knew it was never that easy. We knew too that we had more or less finished our food. Our rations would be nothing more than melted snow from here on in. That did not concern us at all. We were only a few hours from the summit and, as long as we did not suffer with altitude problems during the night, and the weather stayed fair, the summit should be in the bag. I went to sleep with a quiet confidence, tucked securely inside the flanks of Nanga Parbat.

PART 3
THE SUMMIT

08

IN SOME LOST PLACE

Morning broke on our fourteenth day on the mountain, 15 July. It was freezing and I felt it. Two weeks in the thin air of altitude. Days since we had eaten anything substantial. No wonder I was cold. Digging a snow cave in down clothing is a bad idea; we knew that perfectly well and had tried not to overheat the night before. Even so, our jackets and trousers had become damp with perspiration as we struggled in the confined space of the snow cave. Rick's gloves were frozen solid, mine partly so. The clothing I had hidden against my body was dry enough, and my gloves were at least usable, but Rick's were like two frozen fish. He pulled them on to his hands but I could see from his expression that they were not insulating him very well.

Now we were on the edge of things, feeling apathetic but encouraging each other to keep going. Fighting the frustration of trying to adjust the sliders on our zips with frozen gloves. Endeavouring to be brave. Fourteen days now, much of it spent at 7,000 metres and above, climbing the Mazeno, that amazing knife-edge ridge in the sky. How wonderful it felt; our commute to work was enviably free of traffic. It was satisfying to know that we had it all to ourselves. But I was still plagued by doubts from yesterday. Why could we not see any signs of other climbers on the Kinshofer?

We had no intention of letting these minor frustrations stop us from stomping on to the summit. And thanks to the efficiency of the Sumo stoves we only had a short wait to get some warm water to drink. Then we were stuffing all our gear into the sacks and crawling out of the cave into another bright blue day at altitude.

From our experience in 2009 we knew the way was not easy; we had some boulders to surmount and lots of rock to scramble over. I thought I could remember the gist of it.

We cleared the snow cave and took everything we had with us in our sacks. In those first hours it was tough going, up steep snow where we had to kick our feet in hard. We came to the point where the steeper slopes rounded off and the terrain became rockier, but in this season of heavy snow I still had to break trail between the bigger boulders. We would sink in and get our feet caught between rocks, so we tried to step from boulder to boulder. Often the protruding stones were too far apart and we would sink through the snow's crust. The mist came down and visibility was poor; occasionally we would stop and check to see if we both thought we were going in the right direction. Conversation was minimal; we just wanted to reach the top.

At every step we had to lift each foot high out of our boot prints and then sink them down again, each one an immense effort, like dragging your foot out of treacle. We swapped leads but only occasionally. We'd each do long periods in front. Time seemed to speed up, the simple act of placing one foot in front of the other taking an age. The morning slipped past. We found ourselves on more awkward ground, and there was a cool breeze now. It was still misty, so we couldn't see much ahead. At 2 p.m. we were on a rounded summit. I felt certain we were in the right place, but there was no sign of the discarded odds and ends I had seen in 2009, a piece of aluminium T-bar and a length of wire, which mark the summit. I searched around, scuffing at the summit with my foot, but the markers eluded me. I also knew the rock features were not quite what I remembered.

Through the mist we could see vaguely a series of bumps, a kind of castellated ridge and so we walked over that way and kept going, but knew that we were moving lower and our efforts were being wasted. We were close but not close enough. There was a brief window in the cloud, and we saw a higher point and made for it. Then the mist closed in again. We wanted to dump our rucksacks but knew that in the mist we might not find them again.

We worked our way along, losing height and then climbing up to small summits. Eventually we had stood on several. It reminded me of searching for the Ordnance Survey's trig point on Lochnagar in the mist. Time just drained away and somehow it was 5 p.m. The day was gone. We had been above 8,000 metres for hours and I was exhausted. Eventually I suggested to Rick just to take photos of us on one of the mini-summits.

'Really, who cares anyway?' I felt completely dejected and wholly demoralised; I no longer cared about the actual summit. We took out our cameras but locating the little shutter buttons was freezing our hands. We knew we had walked some distance from the real summit, probably hundreds of metres, so we turned around and headed back, thinking it was all over and all we could do was descend unrewarded.

At that point the mist suddenly lifted, the air cleared and it felt as though the last of the sun was about to break through. We could see higher ground now and climbed up towards it. As the mist finally dissipated we recognised the summit. I was exhausted and almost at the end of my tether. Rick was too, but with all my energy drained from my body, I had to ask him to go in front. Somehow he found the energy to break trail.

Sometimes we found traces of our earlier progress in the snow, and then we would be on virgin ground again until eventually we stood in brilliant evening sunlight on the true summit. The sky was now azure, with hardly a breath of wind. We were being blessed! It was an extraordinary turn of events – because I had given up my summit ambition, I was being granted it. Our persistent seeking had turned our fortunes. On the snow beside the summit rocks lay the aluminium bar; its length of wire somehow stuck to the rocks. Recognition dawned in my foggy mind and my face slowly creased into a smile. We were both intensely happy.

I set my camera on some rocks and, carefully lining it up, pressed the shutter and shuffled quickly back to crouch beside Rick. We had our summit shot but took some more. Rick tried to get a few of me but, exhausted from the climb to the summit and with his frozen gloves, the results were forgivably poor. He didn't much care about such things anyway. Rick and I have climbed for years together and there are almost zero photos of me. I persevered and took as many photos as I could, trying to frame the shot as well as I was able. We had climbed the Mazeno Ridge all the way to the top. We had climbed a new line on Nanga Parbat, a British line. Or should we call it the Scottish route?

I felt deeply emotional. I was thinking of my daughters at home. I was thinking of Doug Scott, who had first introduced me and Rick to this ridge, and of Voytek Kurtyka, who I always thought would be with us when we did it. I thought of Cathy and the three Lhakpas; there was no way our success was just ours. Generations of climbers had got us here. I thought that Fred Mummery would be delighted, his ambitious Victorian plan vindicated. From my pocket I pulled out a snotty frozen handkerchief and with it came some spare storm matches and their little cardboard box, now in pieces. They fell on to the main summit block and I thought I should pick them up. But the matchbox was so broken and damp that it fell to pieces in my gloves. I only managed to recover a few matches and some fragments of the box and left the rest. 'That's a silly thing to do,' I thought.

I wanted to stay and take more photos but Rick was pushing to leave. We probably spent fifteen minutes on the summit and then made our way down. It was obvious then that we had to get back to the snow cave. It was now after 6 p.m. and all of a sudden the wind was blowing and night was falling; the benign summit was changing into one of the most hostile places on Earth. We tried to delay putting on our head torches but eventually darkness forced us to stop and dig them out. It began to snow as I was looking for our line of tracks coming up, and I found a trace of them eventually. I tried to follow them with the beam of my head torch. Then I peered behind me to make sure Rick was following.

We were still roped up, but the place felt isolated and imposing. I felt as though death was following in our steps, lurking just out of sight. It frightened me, and so I looked around, checking my friend was still there. We were the only two people in the world, alone in this hellish place of windblown snow and darkness. I dug deep inside myself, thinking how it was only as bad as the Cairngorm plateau in a whiteout on a freezing January night. I could feel energy from Rick, willing me to stay on course and find the snow cave. I kept moving, sometimes steeply downhill, plunging my boots into the snow, searching frantically for a hint of our upward track. Like an albatross on the Southern Ocean, I simply followed my natural navigational instincts over the wide expanse of snow and finally came to the cave. Relief washed over me. Finally we could escape the wind and driving snow. Soon we would be inside our sleeping bags and, with luck, the temperature inside would be closer to zero and we would be fine.

Often on these grand summits in the Himalaya you get everything thrown at you, as though the spirits or mountain gods want to test you just one more time. It's vital to stay calm and do things right, to have the inner confidence to keep following the rules. When that peace of mind leaves you, when you panic or cut corners, that's when you lose it. So far I have been lucky. I have too many friends who have not had such luck. Now I felt like we'd escaped with moments to spare.

Inside our cave it was relatively calm; the anxiety and turmoil of struggling through the dark became a memory. The thick white walls of our home muffled the sound of the wind. Inside our sleeping bags, the cave entrance half-closed with our rucksacks, Rick went to light the stove. Nothing doing. He tried again. His lighter wasn't working. It didn't offer a single spark. He searched his pockets for a spare but there was none. My lighter, I knew, had gone down the mountain with Cathy.

I remembered my storm matches and found them in the deepest corner seams of my down clothing, but the box was ruined and the little emery strip gone. I thought of the summit and could see in my mind's eye an action replay of that flick of my frozen handkerchief throwing out the dilapidated cardboard matchbox. Bugger, I thought. Surely we can strike these matches on something? We considered the abrasive surfaces available. Nothing doing. Our food had completely gone the night before. We had finished our water during the climb to the summit and were now unable to melt snow for more.

We decided sleep was more important and we would address the problem again in the morning. It would only be one more day. We should be able to get down to Base Camp by the following night. We'd sleep and try harder to light the stove in the morning. I changed my socks and then jammed my rucksack more carefully into the cave entrance to prevent too much spindrift from blowing in, while still allowing a breath of air to enter so we didn't suffocate. From inside his sleeping bag Rick sent a text to Samandar using the satellite phone to say that we had summited, were okay and would be heading down the Kinshofer route in the morning. To save the battery, he kept the message short and quickly turned the phone off again. Both satisfied we had done enough, we settled down to sleep. I was comatose in minutes.

The next morning the usual ritual started: reach out of the sleeping bag, light the stove and put on a pan of snow. Only we still couldn't get the lighter to spark. We tried again and again. Nothing doing. Rick's lighter seemed completely dead. In the cold light of day, our situation became frighteningly clear. We were already dehydrated from our climb, and now there was no prospect of water. It was a disaster. Dehydration at these altitudes can soon debilitate the body. Blood thickens to treacle. The risk of stroke or some other dangerous condition was very real.

Rather than let these fears overwhelm us, we decided it was simply best to get our boots on and start moving down the mountain. I thought about our descent in 2009. Two or three hours would get us down to the site of Camp 4. It was then another two hours to Camp 3, and another two to Camp 2 at around 6,300 metres. The air would be thicker there. The afternoon sun would be shining there. We would be able to take our gloves off and fiddle with the stove. I thought too that we would likely meet climbers attempting the Kinshofer route. There would be tent platforms dug out in the snow and people with stoves and masses of food. The priority was to keep moving down; we had to escape this death zone.

In the freezing cold it took us a while to get ready. It felt as though the air was scalding my face as I squeezed out of the narrow entrance of the snow cave. I breathed cautiously through the fabric of my neck scarf, filling my lungs. It felt refreshing, like an advert for spearmint gum. The sky was overcast and I assessed the weather for a moment: not great. I discussed it with Rick as I stood first on one leg and then the other to clip on my crampons. I felt okay but was desperate to get moving.

Rick's mittens were frozen and it took ages for us both to do the simplest things. I struggled to fasten my parka zip, and threading the buckle of my lightweight climbing harness was causing havoc with my fingernails; it was always desperately difficult to tease the faded orange belt through the double buckle. I had to hold it apart with my fingers, and in the cold tore the top off my nail. Blood seeped up from the wound and I cursed in pain. Harnesses on, I shouldered my rucksack. All these simple tasks had become an exhausting hassle in our state of hypoxic exhaustion. It's now you really find out just how well designed climbing gear is. I am not a fan of fiddly zips or hoods with trendy pull-cord adjusters. Fiddling with these at extreme altitude can mean setting your fingers up for amputation.

I began to wonder whether what we were doing was humanly possible. We had climbed the Mazeno and reached the summit, but we both knew that we had wasted too much energy searching out the top in the misty conditions. In among conflicting emotions, exhaustion and elation, we both knew that our bodies could not sustain this amount of time at altitude for much longer, especially now we had no water. The slow trickle of attrition had turned into a flood; it was simply a matter of time before our bodies went into spasm and simply stopped functioning. Which one of us would succumb first? Would the other have enough energy to get both of us down to thicker air?

We roped up, more from force of habit and camaraderie than necessity, although it made carrying the rope easier. It didn't take us long to realise the going was slow, painfully slow. For long sections of the descent the snow was a firm slab, the frustrating sort that almost supports your weight but, just as you weight it, breaks, and your leg sinks into the powder beneath, in this case up to our knees and sometimes thighs. It made it all desperately hard work. Pulling my foot up would bring a chunk of slab with it, and that would begin to slide, giving us something else to trip over.

Rick led the way but had to rest constantly; walking was awkward and exhausting. I offered to take over for a bit. It was tediously slow and hours drifted by in a kind of featureless silence. We were too tired to engage with one another and seemed to be making hardly any progress at all. The ground was quite steep and we curved our way around in a long S-shaped arc that would lead us to the site of Camp 4 on the Kinshofer. The weather deteriorated, clouds inflated powerfully in the sky above and snow began to fall. So much for my weather prediction, I thought. Rick had a compass in the top pocket of his sack so we stopped and he pulled it out. We sat on our sacks while I estimated a bearing from my rudimentary map and sketchy memory of the last time we were there. Then we shouldered our sacks again, just as the cloud enveloped us and the snow fell more heavily.

The situation felt serious. Rick started talking, but his words made no sense at all. It was gibberish, language I can't put down on the page. I wondered how exhausted he was. He seemed to have become deranged and emotional. He berated himself. Was our predicament overwhelming him? Had his body been so wrung out of all its fluids that his mind was about to give in? I hoped that it couldn't happen that quickly, but then I didn't really know. I'd been exhausted before but I'd never been so long at altitude without food or water. I had no idea how quick our demise might be.

I remembered Doug telling me about our mutual friend Pete Thexton on Broad Peak, how during their ascent he had been doing fine and telling everyone that he was doing fine and then within minutes he had collapsed. Doug and the rest of the team had to administer first aid and begin sledging him down in the hope that thicker air might revive him. It was no good. Pete died, and the aftermath of his loss rippled outwards through the community and down the years. I knew really that our bodies could give up very quickly at altitude. I was intensely aware that we had both pulled out all the stops reaching the summit. From somewhere, Rick had found the extra energy to lead us back up to the summit a second time, but doing so must have burnt up every last ounce of his willpower and energy. Since then we had had nothing to eat or drink.

I forced myself to think methodically about our situation and how to bring Rick safely down the mountain. We had been running on empty, surviving on adrenaline and hope, and now all we had to do to reach safety was slog down a relatively straight-forward descent route. We had climbed together so much over the years that I felt confident there was not a single part of Rick that would easily surrender, give up or let me down. But I had never heard him talking so unintelligibly in the past. Rick's mind was running away from him and not making any sense. Then I wondered if I was at fault. Was I misconstruing his words? We were both after all in the same predicament, running on the same nothingness. Maybe my brain was the one that was losing it? Maybe, but I didn't think so.

'Hey Rick, I have no idea what you are on about, but you'd better pull your mind together as you are not making any sense. It's upsetting for me too.' I spoke quite firmly to him, trying to show Rick that while I understood his difficulties I also needed him to realise he was behaving strangely, just like you tell your ski-buddy his nose is turning white with early signs of frostbite on a freezing day. He had to fight to keep things together and regain control of his emotions so we could keep descending. It's not easy telling your best pal, who you know to be incredibly strong, that he is talking nonsense. But Rick apologised and I hoped my message had got through to him. I told him not to worry and we carried on descending. It was quiet now, except for the snowflakes landing on our hoods and the whoosh of our footsteps in the snow. We struggled in silence, bound together by a nine-millimetre cord of hope, a team that was running on empty.

Eventually the snow was falling so heavily that visibility reduced to a whiteout. I followed my estimated bearing, feeling the angle of the terrain under my feet and trying to equate that to my memories of the mountain from four years ago. I called on myself to focus, to draw on all that knowledge, to imagine myself in the Cairngorms in a howling wind. I navigated onward, sensing Rick stepping along behind me on the occasionally taut rope. After what felt like an age of deep snow and exhausting effort, we came to the bowl just above the site of the Kinshofer's Camp 4. Rick was with me in body but it was clear his mind had gone elsewhere. He kept wanting to stop and so I set an even slower pace, hoping he could keep going, allowing us both to continue moving. It felt obvious to me even in the limited visibility that traversing down to Camp 4 would be foolhardy in such bad snow conditions. New snow was accumulating at a fast rate and it was possible we might trigger an avalanche on this lower-angled terrain.

I opted to take a slightly higher line and maintained this, gently skirting the contour one would normally take to reach Camp 4. In my mind I was making for the edge of the unseen bowl, where

I knew we would be away from any terrain traps, and where eventually the snow would thin to rock. From that very edge in 2009 we had sat on rocks and enjoyed the views together before descending. It was an idyllic spot in good weather, and while it could be exposed to the wind, that at least meant the snow would be blown clear and we could see its obvious physical features, even in this poor visibility. It would also be relatively safe to stop and rest there. So, despite the whiteout, I would be able to figure out exactly where we were when we reached it.

We both needed a break and Rick stopped when I did, half-slumping on his sack. I pulled out the satellite phone and tried to make a call. My mind was so weary, it took a while to free my fingers and work the keypad. I tried to compose myself so I didn't sound desperate and knew what I wanted to say as quickly as possible so I didn't waste the battery. I told Rick I would talk to Ali and tell him about the snow conditions and how concerned I was. I said I would ask him about the availability of a helicopter. I didn't want a rescue at this stage, but I thought it would be prudent to ask if one could be available if required. Then I dialled the number and it felt like a miracle when Ali picked up. The relief on hearing his voice was intense, and I had to fight to control my emotions. I didn't feel the need to ask him how the weather was, but he passed on his congratulations.

I asked if Cathy and the three Lhakpas were okay and he said they were back in the Shangrila in Chilas. I had a sudden image of them, washed and dressed in clean clothes, relaxing at a well-polished dining-room table, eating roast chicken and fresh vegetables. I told him the phone battery was fading and confirmed our intention to descend the Kinshofer. I asked if our approach shoes and some valley clothing could be sent to the Diamir Base Camp, perhaps with our Sherpas if they had the energy. Ali said the Sherpas were exhausted and would not be able to assist at all. But he would organise some local high-altitude porters to come with our clothing and some food. I also asked him what the helicopter situation was. Ali asked if we needed one. I said no, but that we were out of water and food and our bodies were deteriorating fast. Even if we were okay for now, I am sure he could tell from my strained voice that the situation was far from okay. He told me what I knew already, that the helicopters could not fly that high and the weather was cloudy. There was no chance just now.

I told him that if we needed a helicopter it would be later, and that if I thought that was likely I would call him. Whatever happened, we would keep going down and try to finish the climb under our own steam. I reminded him that we had paid the helicopter bond and he confirmed that. We didn't want to spend it, but would do so if our situation became life or death. Ali said he would check about helicopter availability but would hold off committing to one just yet. Ali also confirmed that he would try to get some porters to Diamir Base Camp and maybe to Camp 1. I asked him if he knew whether other climbers were trying to climb the Kinshofer. He said he didn't know but assumed there were.

Ali also told me that we were making big news back home and that people were thinking we were having an epic. He had spoken to my sister Eunice. I said we were doing fine and when speaking to people it was probably best simply to say we were making our way down and that communication was difficult as there was little battery power for our phone. I told Ali we were tired and Rick had been a little bit out of it. I said I would try and phone at 5 p.m. to let him know if we wanted a helicopter, but otherwise all was fine. Then we hung up and I was back on the mountain, beyond outside help.

Rick had heard most of this conversation and we discussed it. Now he understood that I was really concerned for him. Prior to the call, he had wanted to stop all the time. He was still periodically speaking gibberish. His walking was ungainly; he'd lost that neat sense of purpose he usually has on a mountain. Rick's body was often slumped over his axe, his sack hanging to one side on his shoulders, his coiled rope a tangle of spaghetti. I was aware that I was probably becoming a little bedraggled too. But I thought I was doing well enough and it did seem that my awareness of our situation was higher. While I was finding it desperately hard, I felt I still had my act together and if I could maintain it then Rick could do too.

It was now about 3 p.m. and within an hour I had broken trail to the edge of the rim. I told Rick I thought we should bivouac here. We had used up nearly all the day just getting to this point and given the avalanche risk below it made more sense to tackle what lay beneath in the morning when we may be able to see something. At least we would be safe here. If the weather cleared, with luck we would get a long way down the next day. Rick agreed and we wandered about a bit until we found a mound of snow in which we could dig a shelter for the night. Despite being on the move all day, we had only descended to about 7,400 metres.

We started digging into the snow mound, again with the adzes of our ice axes, burrowing from opposite sides of the mound with the aim of meeting in the middle. We would then carve out more snow and close up one of the entrances. Eventually we would have a fine cave to shelter in and lie down, a proverbial pocket of paradise. I set to work and after about two hours I was well inside, having carved out a big cave. I kept expecting to see Rick's ice axe appearing through the snow from his side, but it didn't happen. I was just starting to think that I had better go and see what he was up to when I heard Rick's desperately pleading voice: 'Sandy, Sandy, can I please get into your cave. It's hopeless, really hopeless.' His voice was high and coming from behind me, rather than from the direction of his tunnel. I stopped and turned around. I could just see his legs and boots outside the entrance of my tunnel. I reversed out of the cave and stood up, looking into his face. He looked fragile and exhausted, his head wrapped tightly in the hood of his down jacket.

'It's okay Rick, of course you can, no worries.' I wondered why he said it was my cave and not ours. 'Tell me what's wrong?' I felt my heart quicken as I saw the distress in his eyes. 'It's hopeless, just hopeless. I was digging for ages. The snow is hopeless, it's all collapsed in and I have got nothing done.' I felt incredibly anxious that my climbing pal was losing his marbles. 'We can both squeeze into the side I've dug, no problem. I'll go around and see if I can do anything where you've been working.' I showed him where he could dig on my side, and he got on to his knees, crawled forward and began to burrow.

When I looked at his side of the snow-hump I could see only a few trivial scrapes on the very surface of the snow. He had dug nothing at all. Rick had been standing there in the open for two hours, just waving his ice axe around in the air, occasionally catching the top surface of the snow bank. His frustration at the collapsing snow hole was probably just the fantasy of a mind on the edge of collapse. It all felt so serious to me; I felt very alone and isolated and the real vulnerability of our position filled my thoughts. Dealing with such things on a pre-planned winter snow-caving expedition to the Cairngorm plateau at 3,000 feet is tough enough. But here we were, still above 7,000 metres, out of food for days and water for thirty-six hours.

I wondered if I had enough strength left to face up to all this. I recalled the first aid ABC motto – airway, breathing, circulation – that I'd adapted years ago: ALWAYS – BE – COOL. I knew my own body was deteriorating too; the lack of drinking water and the strength needed to plough a trail through the deep snow compounded the time at high altitude. Digging a snow shelter with the tiny head of my ice axe required massive amounts of energy. If Rick was going down I must be too. It was simply a matter of time before we were both in an unavoidable decline and ground to a halt. I wondered how long that would take, but then realised I was seeing it already.

Then again, perhaps reflecting on this persistent uncertainty would destabilise my morale. The constant recycling of potential threats in my mind could lead to a mental state that stopped me from making sound decisions. Perhaps this was what had happened to Rick? I began to wonder if the decisions I had already made were sensible after all.

Darkness was on its way, it was chilly and I had only dug about three-quarters of our cave. I braced myself mentally and walked back round to my entrance, taking care to place my feet carefully. I watched the snowflakes fall and found myself mentally assessing the impact the current weather would have on the snowpack. I marvelled at the incredible dendritic shapes of the flakes as they lay on the fabric of my sleeve. I felt the wind on my skin. I noticed that I noticed myself, a magnified me, reading these signs. It was like being back on the hill above Sheffield with my pal Mark Miller, watching dawn strike the city, our minds stretched to the horizon.

Everything simply stopped for a moment and I saw nature at its wildest and best. I felt a realisation that something profound was happening. God stocktaking, I thought, ticking a list, two humans on the side of the mountain. I felt suddenly lifted up spiritually, encouraged and reassured. I felt totally at home in this wild environment. I was acutely aware of our exposure and my deep fear, but I felt I was now receiving some positive energy too, nature reassuring me that I was aware and had the skills and experience to handle all that was happening. I felt strong and absolutely convinced I could do what I needed to. I don't know where it came from, but I knew I had the strength to continue.

09

THE EDGE OF EXTINCTION

I half crawled through the small entrance tunnel of our rudimentary shelter and suggested Rick reverse out and get our rucksacks while I enlarged the cave a bit more. I dug away for a bit, cleared the loose snow from the floor and called out to him, 'this'll be great.' Then I crawled out and suggested he go back inside so I could pass him the sacks. It was dark now and the sweat on my body from digging was starting to freeze in the bitter night air. I passed in the rucksacks and squeezed in beside him.

Rick managed to climb into his sleeping bag and at last I got into mine. His body and legs were inside the cave, while my torso was sheltered from the worst of the wind but my legs stuck out; we would also benefit from the cave ceiling above us retaining any heat. The roof was also big enough to deflect any spindrift that might otherwise cover our bodies. I was still feeling positive and, while concerned for our precarious position, happy enough. I remembered the words of Scottish mountaineer Tom Patey, who was famous for soloing technically hard winter climbs and had a reputation as a party animal. He wrote many famous songs and poems about the climbing world. There was always a good craic in Highland pubs and mountain bothies when Tom played his harmonica. One of his songs, The Last of the Grand Old Masters, describing my hero Joe Brown, came to mind: 'I am the last of the grand old masters/But now I am old and grey/When the sweat on my neck turns to verglas/You will find I have passed away.'

I mumbled the words out loud and relaxed a little as the verglas on my neck started to melt. I did my sock-change routine and tried to get the stove going again. Rick had tucked the cylinder inside his sleeping bag in the hope the gas would warm up slightly. While excavating the snow cave I had collected some small dry stones and had them warming in the inside pocket of my down parka. Holding them in my hand and sheltering my hand with my body to block out the spindrift, I prepared to light the stove, now reassembled. I tried to spark my storm matches off the small dry stones but they refused to spark. Sometimes I got a hopeful sulphur-like smell and a lick of smoke curling up from the match, but even with the gas turned on and almost choking us there was never enough of a spark to ignite a flame.

Rick suggested breaking apart the lighter to get to the fuel inside. It seemed like a good idea but we both realised doing so would be a final desperate throw of the dice. When I broke it open I saw that the flint had completely worn away. So that's why it wouldn't work. I sprinkled the remaining lighter fluid on the stove's burner and tried to get the matches to spark on to it but even this failed. It was typical of us to have brought a half-used lighter. We'd used it on a previous expedition and found it in our gear cache. I decided to keep my views on thrift quiet since I hadn't carried a spare lighter myself, leaving that to Cathy. Such was our fate and there was no option but to accept it.

So that was it. Our attempts to light the stove were over. We had to accept that melting snow for water was not going to happen, dehydration was inevitable and rather than focus our energies on negative thoughts, we had to combat our emotions and not let it frustrate us. People asked me afterwards what my throat was like after so long without water. To be honest, I didn't think about it. I couldn't allow myself to. There was nothing to be done except put all the discomfort to the back of my mind. It served no purpose to dwell on it. We huddled together inside our respective sleeping bags, switched off our head torches to save the batteries and simply lay there in the spindrift and the darkness.

Rick seemed calmer and more at ease. We acknowledged we had made incredibly slow progress that day. Neither of us had experienced such deep and difficult snow for such long stretches in all our years of climbing; the descent had simply eaten up time. We could not have done any better.

There was no hint of negativity between us. We accepted that the situation dominated us rather than us being in control but, despite this, we buoyed each other up with positive plans for the morning. We fostered the hope that tomorrow we would get down to Camp 1 or maybe even Base Camp and all would be fine. I rearranged our sleeping bags and placed our rucksacks over our legs, trying to prevent the spindrift from building up over our chests, and wished Rick a good night. I cracked a joke about achieving the ultimate in eco-friendly aspirations; no one could criticise us for using up resources and causing pollution. We had nothing to exploit.

It took a while to sleep and my thoughts drifted to my daughters Hannah and Cara. I wondered what they were up to, what adventures were occurring in their lives. I felt a responsibility to get home to them, not that they needed me from a material sense. I wondered what state we would be in by daylight tomorrow. I recalled the words of my ex-wife Janis during our divorce so many years ago. Once our divorce came through, that wildly expensive piece of paper confirming our marriage was over, Jan reminded me how she used to drive me to the station or airport with the kids in the back at the start of yet another expedition with my pals. I would be happy, jolly and waving at them, blowing kisses. Then, as she watched me leaving, holding the small hands of our two beautiful young daughters in her own, she told me she always had the same thought: 'I wonder if he will live through this climb. I wonder if I will see him again?'

I had no idea that she had these thoughts. I wondered whether many Himalayan climbers heading out to try new hard climbs at extreme altitude did. We feel the projects we have in mind are possible and that accidents are unlikely as our skills are adequate. I personally seemed to make good decisions and would not do anything overambitious or silly; and if things got too serious or difficult then I had the skills to retreat. I also knew for certain that if I had even the slightest thought that I could die I would not leave home. I have always been aware that climbing is serious; I often used to say that we climbed serious routes but we were serious people. But while we enjoyed and even relished attempts on these seemingly impossible faces and ridges, the people we left behind had to endure their own incredible internal expeditions and I do not think I truly realised the mental hardship that they went through in my absence.

Now, on Nanga Parbat in the most intense experience of my mountain life, I felt the seriousness of what was happening. The failure to light the stove once more made me acutely aware of our precarious state. I had never seen Rick so weak, so slow-witted. We had climbed the north face of the Eiger together, between seasons, late in October; it was the only time we could get off work. On seeing the snowed-up face we thought we would race up it in a couple of days, so I insisted we lighten our sacks and not take much food or spare clothing. I even left a small pile of food and gas at the foot of the climb.

Once on the face we realised the snow was new and hadn't yet morphed into névé to take an ice axe or crampon points. This made the climbing incredibly awkward. The fresh snow also seemed to worsen the steady showers of stone-fall for which the Eiger is so famous. We climbed the route in fine enough style for the era but ended up having three bivouacs without much food. On the descent Rick had dwindled away, becoming a shadow of his former strength. The same was happening here but more dramatically and in much more arduous circumstances. If he collapsed there would likely be only one outcome. I knew I had to stay strong and give him the impression that all was well and that I could look after him. I wondered if I really had the strength. Even if I didn't, I still had to try.

I pulled the sleeping bag hood over my head and rustled around inside my sleeping bag to shift my clothing so that I had some additional insulation between my hip and the sleeping bag on the frozen snow; my sleeping mat having been abandoned for our push to the summit. My thoughts were warm and happy, and I whispered my nightly prayers. We are just human, overflowing with faults and frailties. I wondered if Rick would wake up or pass away by the morning. I wondered if I would wake up impotent in the face of this relentless high-altitude drama. I reminded myself that it was not a tragedy yet and that I would work as hard as I could to avoid such an event. I wondered about my own faith, acknowledging that I was probably less devout than I should be, but I still carried the feeling of something good watching over me from my spiritual moment earlier.

I dug deep within myself, trying to engage in a serious conversation with myself so that I would hang in, get the job done and see my mate safely off the mountain. I had warm memories of my Sunday school days, the source of my Calvinistic inheritance. Would I be like Jonah, swallowed by the whale but keeping faith, and so eventually be released? Maybe the whale just belched him up. Maybe that sense of mystery was all in my head. I'm used to the intellectual rejection by others of religious feeling. It's easy to justify disbelief, to say there is in fact nothing out there in the dark. I still retained a hunger for Christian expression, a solid connection to the faith I'd experienced as a child. These days, I float somewhere between Buddhism and Christianity, sitting in the middle of life's proverbial rocky road. Rick and I were the human connection here, the fragility of our existence tangible in this inhospitable place. The altitude, the freezing air and the snows of the killer mountain could easily snuff us out. We were in this together, huddling in this hopeless shelter as a warm glow suffused my weary body and I drifted into a sound sleep.

The night was cold and cramped. Occasionally I would wake, glancing over to see Rick rustling in his sleeping bag. But we made it through and in the morning I thought I had done well for sleep. I lay there wondering if Rick was okay or whether I would have to drag him all the way to Base Camp. Would he kill us both by not being able to move? I thought of lowering him, of making a mistake and letting him fall, or else being pulled from my stance and joining him in a final horrifying plunge down the mountain. I was awoken from my morbid thoughts by Rick's voice and instantly realised I had nothing to fear. He sounded almost chirpy. Thank goodness, he seemed to be doing well, he seemed re-charged. I was not going to be alone. We both had a common purpose: to get up, get ourselves moving and make a quick exit.

I peered around and discovered we were both covered in spindrift, our feet and legs buried in about half a metre of fine snow that had accumulated during the night. We eased ourselves out with caution, trying our best not to let the powder get inside our sleeping bags or unzipped clothing. At least we didn't have to waste time making a brew or eating breakfast. In what seemed like an instant we had everything packed. Outside, it was cold but clear with a faint breeze and I revelled in our good fortune. I felt a simple connection with this awesome environment.

Looking around us, I could see we were indeed where I thought. The snow slopes above us revealed small avalanches of snow which had crept towards the site of Camp 4. Compared to the last snow cave at 7,720 metres, it felt so much easier to pull on our gloves, tighten our bootlaces and adjust the Velcro closures on our gaiters and wrists. Our path from yesterday, perhaps better described as a trench, was now almost completely obliterated. I could just see the occasional trace of it, but it had more or less been totally filled with falling snow. Clearly there had been quite a dump of snow last night; we would have to be even more aware of avalanches.

We roped up again. In my mind at least I was stronger and so, since we were moving on to very steep ground, I put myself at the back to hold any falls. Rick would climb down in front. He plunged his feet and set off down as I held the rope taut with coils in my sack and a few tied off around my shoulders. I had gone into mountain guide mode; it was simply what I had done for so much of my life. In this lost place, the lyrics to Leonard Cohen's song Teachers came to me as Rick led on down.

Rick was okay and seemed strong, although I sensed his mind had lost focus. I felt that he was being a bit reckless, just ploughing down, no longer thinking about choosing a line, not really considering the subtleties of the terrain, the slope's angle, the types of snow or the bonding of layers.

Then Rick surprised me and made me question myself, made me think I was being complacent. He came to a stop and asked me which way I thought was better. The fact he did so cheered me immensely. I realised he was still alert, partly at least. He still had the ability to think and wanted the two of us to work together; he was thinking of us as a team with a sense of combined efficiency and wellbeing. There remained a balance between our individual capabilities and our mutual willpower. Before he had been simply surviving. Now, with his simple question, it was clear that his continuing silence was simply to conserve his energy and not dehydrate himself further by opening his mouth to the greedy air.

A lot of the time it was hardly necessary for us to consult one another at all, since the ground was steep enough that any fresh snow would slide off as it fell. At times we had to face inwards towards the slope and use our front points to climb down, never needing to stop and safeguard each other, just moving together as before.

We were on the relentless treadmill down, down, down, like prisoners of war forced to keep on digging some impossible road, simply because we had to. It was beginning to feel unfair, even though all of it – the ridge, the summit, even losing our lighter – was under our control. But we had no choice, we had to continue, not because we were being whipped by some well-fed enemy, but because we wanted to live and this was the only way. Our lives depended on us continuing until we got off the mountain.

Not so far away now, I could see that the slope angle was shallower and the chances of us triggering an avalanche seemed far higher. I was convinced that the slope was going to slide and so I shouted to Rick to wait while I stamped my feet into a trench and uncoiled more rope, securing it again at my waist. I thrust my ice axe into the snow beside me and told Rick I was ready for him to move on.

Sure enough, as he reached the change in angle and stepped on it in what seemed to me like semi-reckless abandon, the whole slope slid away in a massive avalanche, cascading down over the uppermost reaches of the Mummery Rib. Rick rolled to the side and I held him tight on the rope. It was like working for the ski patrol, setting off small avalanches without explosives. I thought of my friends in British Columbia who had taught me so much about snowpacks and their layers; I thought of buddies in the Scottish Avalanche Information Service. I'd learned something.

I'm always wary of involvement with snow; it is enigmatic stuff, a dazzling, wonderful, intriguing phenomenon. Dave McClung and Peter Schaerer's *The Avalanche Handbook*, my bible on the subject, would dictate that we should have gone around this area of risk – as would common sense. Bruce Tremper's *Staying Alive in Avalanche Terrain* would definitely question my sanity. But the reality was that if I wanted to avoid this slope we would have needed to climb back up over the summit and descend the Schell. That wasn't going to happen. Nor did we have the resources to dig in and wait in our sleeping bags while the slopes below consolidated. We had no option but to climb down, even if there was a risk that we might be avalanched off the slope. To continue and maybe die, or stay and definitely die – it wasn't a hard decision.

Rick was fine, but a bit shocked that I had used him as an avalanche trigger. I think he realised he was not quite as sharp and attentive to the snow conditions as he might have been, but good luck was on our side. Moreover, I was delighted when we neared the site of Camp 3. That meant we had traversed the very unstable snowpack and only had to worry about slopes avalanching on us from above. That too was a real risk and one we could only hope didn't happen. Speed of travel is imperative in such situations; you know there is a serious risk from objective dangers like avalanches or hanging séracs, but all you can do is respect them and get on with it. Scurrying under such dangers I could almost hear the time bomb ticking; I tried by an act of mental will to slow it down so we could make our escape before the whole thing exploded. We were truly in the lap of the gods.

We still had not seen any other mountaineers on the normal route, but this did at least mean we didn't have to worry about people triggering the slopes above us. Yet I felt immense pressure. As each hour ticked by our physical condition got worse. The irony was obvious – we were surrounded by water, millions of tons of water, all of it frozen. We were still burning calories with every step, but food was now a distant memory. All we had left was the endless process of ploughing through the snow, every step an immense effort we could no longer afford.

Eventually we reached the brow of the gently curving slopes by Camp 3, and as we moved down them I realised I was hallucinating. Nothing was making sense. I couldn't really understand what was happening, but it wasn't at all distressing – quite the opposite. In the rocks way below us, Snoopy, Charlie Brown's cartoon dog from the Schulz comic strip *Peanuts*, was sitting upright and alert on a narrow rock ledge. I thought at first that I was simply looking at a naturally occurring design where ice had frozen into cracks in the rock. But when I looked harder, it was clear as day. There was Snoopy. I found it immensely comforting to know he was there.

The snowpack was slightly less deep here, and there were exposed sections where the snow had been blown clean off, revealing hard, glass-like ice the colour of chromium. Crossing this we had to focus hard so we didn't slip, stabbing in the front points of our crampons to climb down the bottle-smooth surface. Normally there are old fixed ropes here, but we couldn't find any. I remembered from our ascent in 2009 that the fixed ropes had to be moved higher up the mountain to assist climbers on the mountain that year.

One of them was a lovely South Korean lady called Go Mi-Sun, who we nicknamed Miss Go. She had climbed eleven of the 8,000-metre peaks, mostly with supplementary oxygen, and was trying to become the first Korean woman to complete the list. Go Mi-Sun and others from her Korean and Sherpa team had made the summit late in the evening, several hours behind Rick and me. The winds had been terribly strong. While Rick and I lay resting in our tent at Camp 4, we got word that Miss Go's summit team, including the Sherpa and Pakistani high-altitude porters helping her, were benighted and trapped.

We sent some of Gerfried Göschl's porters to go to their assistance, but in the stormy conditions only some of them managed to reach the distressed climbers and pass on Thermos flasks of warm water and food. The Pakistani porters then helped guide the climbers back to Camp 4 by torchlight. The Korean team was exhausted and in quite a bad way. The following morning they slept late and, as a consequence, descended in bright sunshine which only added to the debilitating effect of high altitude on their tired bodies. While traversing this section between camps 3 and 2, Miss Go slipped off the hard ice. I can imagine her frantically trying to stop her fall but gathering speed until she was lost forever, another victim of the killer mountain. Base Camp was a melancholy place after her death.

I tried hard to avoid thinking of Miss Go's pretty smile as I climbed down the glassy ice, taking great care with my crampon placements. Snoopy was still there, on the same rock ledge, smiling at me. Eventually we came to some ridges in the snow's surface which suggested there was something just below the surface. When we dug down with our ice axes we found what we expected, old snow anchors with lengths of frozen fixed rope. The frozen rope was stretched tight, and on easier sections it was simpler for us to climb down, but on steeper sections we tried to dig the ropes out to speed our descent. I would sit on the snow and belay myself and then lower Rick down the presumed line of old fixed ropes while Rick tried to dig them free.

It was a slow and energy-sapping process. At one point the silhouette of a witch flew by on a broomstick. She was as real to me as Rick was on the other end of the rope. I was sure I was going mad. She had a crooked nose and witch's hat, all pointy and twisted and rather reminiscent of Chesterfield's famous crooked church spire. I could still see Snoopy sitting on the ledge of a rock wall below. The hallucinations seemed so real that I took out my camera to take pictures of them. Rick asked me why I was taking so many shots and I did wonder whether I should tell him or not.

Then there was the rabbit. Did I not mention him? I think he was a boy rabbit. He seemed a little bit crazy, alive and alert, mostly off-white or grey in colour. I could clearly see some of the individual black strands of hair that gave him his grey tint. The rabbit seemed to be overflowing with boisterous cheekiness, rather like the White Rabbit in *Alice in Wonderland*. He wore a bright red waistcoat and had a silver pocket watch chain, hence the White Rabbit, which fell in a curve from a buttonhole to his pocket and sometimes glistened and sparkled as it reflected sunlight. He wore a felt hat like the one you imagine Hermann Buhl might have worn on his first ascent of the mountain, the kind of hat one often still sees Austrian mountain climbers wearing. The rabbit's big ears stuck through holes in the rim. I was convinced he was real, until it struck me as strange that he did not wear any boots or crampons!

The rabbit scampered back and forth, criss-crossing our line of descent just behind Rick and so out of his sight. He didn't leave any footprints and I realised that I was concerned for him. Although furry, the rabbit's feet and toes must be freezing without the protection of footwear. As I lowered Rick I kept looking at the rabbit, kept thinking about his frozen paws. Finally my brain figured out that if the rabbit wasn't leaving footprints in the snow then he couldn't be real. Then I realised that the lack of water and my exhaustion were playing havoc with my mind. I was concerned about myself and focused again on the rope and on letting it run carefully through my gloved fingers.

So we went on, with me lowering Rick or both of us climbing down. At times we would thread our rope through the old tat of an anchor we'd excavated and then abseil. Our rope was only fifty metres in length, so by the time we doubled it we could only abseil twenty-five metres at a time. This made for very slow progress, with the threat of avalanches all the while poised above our heads like the Sword of Damocles. We also knew that with every extra minute that passed our starved bodies were deteriorating further. We pushed on with a renewed sense of urgency, frustrated that progress seemed so slow. We felt the time it was taking to uncover the buried frozen ropes was much too much. My toes were becoming increasingly sore and I became aware that they must have been damaged in the cold.

Our extremities were becoming colder and colder, our hands and feet turning numb as our dwindling physical strength was diverted to our cores in a last-ditch attempt to keep us alive. As I kicked my crampon points into hard ice to get a secure footing, my toes felt the pain of each and every impact. Rick was no different, suffering patiently in silence. I still felt okay, apart from worrying about the rabbit, but at the same time I knew I was half out of my mind with exhaustion, dehydration and hypoxia and that my body was struggling.

After what seemed like several hours of agonising slowness we were finally through the steep and exposed part of the descent and came to a flattish but exposed rib, which I remembered well from our 2009 expedition. The sky was darkening, working through a deepening range of blues to a light charcoal, indicating that night was on its way. My nose felt sore and I touched it, realising that it was exposed to the cold air. My neck scarf must have slipped down during the day. I touched it again and as I brought my hand back into view I could see clotted bits of blood and skin on my gloves. This is not going to look cool to my clients when I get back to guiding above Chamonix, I thought. The rabbit had gone now, although when I looked at the rocks Snoopy was still sitting there. I imagined he must have been as agile as a mountain goat to move around like that from ledge to ledge. All afternoon I looked over to check if I could see him; he was always there, sitting on a ledge. But I never saw him actually move.

A mist came down and enveloped us. I said prayers quietly to myself as I carried on down, but no windows opened in the mist this time and I felt a momentary guilt at bargaining with God in this way and then forgetting about him altogether in times of safety. On reaching the end of the flattish rib area I was certain from my memory that at any point now we had to move rightwards to find a small arête. Then our route should take a semi-technical ridge that would lead us to a rib and eventually to the site of Camp 2. Rick said we had to go left instead, but I just knew he was wrong. It was vital that I listened to him and engaged him by asking why he thought that. I wondered if I should tell him that I was experiencing hallucinations, and felt myself a bit of a cheat for not sharing them. I was still sure in my own mind that I was performing more solidly than him; to let him know that I too was losing it might have been very bad for our confidence. Just because my body was failing and my mind was in an altered state didn't mean I couldn't make sound decisions. So I decided it was best to keep Snoopy, the witch and the cheery rabbit all to myself, which actually indicated to me the lunacy of my own logic.

To our left the mist-enshrouded mountainside looked even steeper and more uninviting. I was certain Rick was wrong. To argue with him was also wrong, so I tried to reason with him, saying that I was pretty sure my memory was correct. He admitted he was not so sure. I said that the side he was proposing dropped off steeply into quite wild, incredibly steep and avalanche-prone terrain. I was filled with a sense of foreboding, and became even more certain that my way was correct. After the snow-cave digging I felt that I could no longer trust his decisions, but knew I couldn't say as much; a hurtful choice of words from me and we could find ourselves in a spiral of disenchantment that would only undermine us further. I felt so guilty not telling him about my hallucinations; I wasn't being very fair. How could I be sure that my usual disciplined approach was holding while my brain was doing such strange things?

Visibility was almost zero. We could now only see perhaps a metre or so in front of us and the terrain was very steep, so I suggested that rather than argue we should bivouac and make the decision when we could see again. Rick agreed even though we were on steep, exposed ground and the site for Camp 2 must have been only two or three hundred metres below us. We also knew that if there was anyone else on the mountain they would quite likely have camped there already. That would have been a blessing, to find a well-stocked tent. I would have had no qualms in borrowing a shelter and melting some snow on their stove. There might even be food. As it was, we were right on the crest of a steep slope. If the wind got up during the night we would be very exposed. Not to continue, to instead face the night without any shelter or anything to drink, was a bleak decision to have to make. It would be our third night without liquid.

Worse, this time, to our mutual disappointment, there was no plump bank of snow in which to dig a cave. Instead we dug a shelf from the powder snow and soon hit glassy, tungsten-hard ice. We placed our single ice screw and tied the centre of the rope into it so we could each have an end. The rest of the rope we coiled as insulation between us and our sleeping bags and the snow. Eventually we got ourselves reasonably comfortable. Rick got into his sleeping bag in a sitting position and I into mine. But I soon realised I wouldn't be able to remain upright all night. So I packed my bag away again and remodelled my side of the snow ledge. Once I'd struggled back into my bag I was able to lay down, at least partially. When the time came to at least try to sleep I could actually elevate my feet and legs.

It was an exposed spot, but the mist obscured the view so that hardly mattered. At least there was more oxygen now, as we were at around 6,300 metres. We were very tired, wholly exhausted, and I knew that my body would drift away to sleep – I have an incredible knack of sleeping anywhere. Yet this time I really did wonder if I would wake up in the morning. My religious nature gave me confidence that I would, but at one point in the night I found myself in a spiritual fairyland, dreaming that I floated on cotton-wool clouds that seemed like heaven. Even when I woke with frozen legs, I wasn't alarmed. I sensed I would be okay whatever happened. I felt there was nothing to fear, just a peaceful calm that would endure forever. While I massaged some warmth back into my cold thighs I reflected on my life, my disciplined childhood, my years of climbing. We chose to do this. I was glad I wasn't here for any other reason – like fame or to please a sponsor. When Rick and I pushed on to the summit we knew full well that once we had chosen to take that path then anything could happen. It was part of why we chose to continue rather than descend with the Sherpas and Cathy. It was what Rick and I had signed up for. Despite the hardships – the bone-aching cold, the terrible thirst – I wanted to be here, whatever the price might be. I was glad I had spent my life free in the mountains.

These thoughts, that my life was ending, sparked something inside me. I pushed them away and concentrated on gently slapping either side of my freezing legs inside my sleeping bag and willing heat to return to my frozen toes. We had to get lower. We were almost out of time.

10

DESCENT

A semblance of warmth began to enter my legs and some even returned to my toes. Cheered by this, I looked over at Rick, who I sensed was also awake. He sat quiet and upright, his sleeping bag's hood shrouding his face. There was absolutely no movement from him. I was concerned, but there was little I could do except think positively and try to ignore the strangeness in my head and the aching cold. Before settling in for the night, I'd had enough discipline to repeat my sock routine and put my outer boots in a big grey refuse sack that I used inside my rucksack to keep things dry. Rucksacks are never waterproof, whatever manufacturers say. Then I'd taken off my inner boots and flattened them so I could slide them under my backside as insulation against the ice. When my toes got too cold, I'd put them back on to warm my feet.

I learned tricks like these in my days with the Cairngorm Mountain Rescue Team. Going out in the arctic Cairngorms when most climbers were coming off the hill after their day's climbing taught me a lot. I sat on the side of Nanga Parbat thinking about my old pals from those days. I saw them now, faces muffled in hoods and woolly hats: Roger Gaff, Willie Anderson, Donnie Williamson and the others. More often than not we were heading out to frozen, inert bodies which we had to stretcher off the hill in the middle of the Cairngorm night. I dozed off thinking of those past times; how there was nothing new in any of this. I'd been here before.

I woke abruptly and struggled upright, removing my inner boots, one at a time, and wriggling my toes furiously inside my sleeping bag. I adjusted the knot on the rope holding me to the belay anchor so it was semi-tight and I could hang there safely. I flipped the hood of my sleeping bag back over my head and pulled the draw cords tight, enclosing my face. Then I tried to sleep again. I was very aware of Rick opposite me. He still sat like a zombie, wrapped in his sleeping bag and bolt upright. I knew he was fading away. I knew his feet and legs would freeze if he remained in that position; we both knew our blood would be as thick as sludge by now. There was no way his heart would have the power to pump blood around his body and down to his feet in that position. I had suggested that he try to lie down or raise his legs a bit but he mumbled he was fine. I asked if he had changed his socks and he replied no, he was keeping his boots on. I suggested he at least slacken off his bootlaces. Again he said he was fine. I knew he wasn't but I didn't want to lecture him.

I was amazed that I slept for quite long periods. When I woke up I was absolutely freezing and I would make small cycling movements with my legs to get some warmth back. This seemed to help and I'd drift off again until I was too cold to sleep, and then the whole process would begin once more. When I was awake I would watch Rick in the darkness, still cocooned in his upright position, having apparently not moved since the last time I'd woken. I assumed he was still conscious, wishing the time away, waiting for dawn. It was a long vigil.

Eventually morning did come. Now fully awake, I waited patiently as the light swung from indigo to blue, to the colours of morning. We started moving at the same time, struggling into the day and packing up in no time at all. We seemed to be okay. I had pains putting on my boots; my toes were frozen, but I sensed they had not yet turned to dead wood and that if we got back to Base Camp that day I might not lose them. Rick said his toes did feel like dead wood and had done so for a while. It wasn't surprising. We had last had a drink three days before. Seventy-two hours without fluid. We hadn't eaten properly in almost a week. Our bodies were eating themselves; our blood, thick and viscous, had crawled into our very cores, preserving our brains and our pumping hearts. Our organs would be starved now of oxygen and energy, on the brink of collapse. Our legs and arms were being sacrificed.

I took a grip of my emotions and tried to shut out this useless mental chatter. I needed control now, not rabbits in red waistcoats. I felt I was living a very simple truth. There was just one thought in my head – that we had to get down to thicker air as soon as possible, before we were undone. There was nothing for me to do but smile and keep going. I touched my nose and flinched, remembering that the day before it had been exposed to the sun and cold. I recalled the blood on my fingers, but it was pointless to care too much about it. I pulled my scarf up and breathed through the improvised facemask.

The mist had lifted and it was a fine enough morning. In my mind I rehearsed the route. I was absorbed in the present. Diamir Base Camp was miles below. We had first to traverse the tricky ridge below to Camp 2. The hope that we might find some tents there still lingered in my mind. Beyond Camp 2 was the difficult Kinshofer Wall. We would need to abseil this, and I knew that in 2009 there had been a massive tangle of fixed ropes up it. Given our experience yesterday, those fixed ropes could well be frozen and useless, but at least we had our own fifty-metre rope with us. Even though the abseils would be short, there would be adequate anchors and we would get down it safely.

From the bottom of the wall there was then a long ice slope to down-climb, which would take us to the gaping bergschrund half concealed with avalanche debris. Once we crossed that we could traverse around to the buttress that sheltered Camp 1 from the séracs and avalanches that often fell from high above. Three to five hours after that we would arrive at Base Camp – easy really, except that in 2009 the route was fixed and we were well watered and fed. I tried to convince myself it would be okay, but I knew full well that in these circumstances it would be extremely hard labour. I wondered whether I would be dragging Rick or if he would be dragging me. Would our bodies simply run out of time?

From our bivouac I climbed down through some rocks, taking monumental care with each front-point placement. I fixed a thread anchor, abseiled, and then held the ends of the rope as Rick followed me and we roped up again. We were now on the ridge leading to Camp 2 at 6,200 metres and when we got there I felt we'd passed an important milestone. There were no tents at all, but by now we were not surprised or disappointed to discover this. We were pleased to see the remains of some tent platforms, an indication that people had at least been there in the last few weeks. At one of the tent platforms we took off our rucksacks and sat on them for a rest. The sun was shining intensely and it was incredibly warm. All of a sudden my mind seemed to shift up a gear. I felt more alert and lucid than I had for days.

This was the first warm sunshine we'd experienced since the lighter failed. We could put snow in our water bottles and use the sun's warmth to melt it. I was amazed I hadn't thought of this before, but the temperatures had been so low it just hadn't occurred to me. We had very occasionally put snow in our mouths to moisten them a little, but it was ultimately no answer to the harsh thirst in our throats. I half-filled my clear plastic bottle with snow, lay it in the sun and joined Rick who was already fast asleep. I slept for maybe ten minutes, woke up with a start and felt slightly rejuvenated but still debilitated. Then I drank a mouthful of slushy snowmelt from the bottle. The sensation of fluid in my throat was delicious. Never had a drink of water tasted so good. I refilled the bottle with snow and while it was melting took off my down clothing, pulled on my Power Stretch underwear and repacked my rucksack. Then I simply sat in the sun.

I felt incredibly grateful and content, sitting on that remote eagle's nest high above the valley. Life couldn't have been more simple or pure. I thought of my daughters. Sometimes I would ask them: 'Hey girls, what are you doing?' They would reply: 'Oh, we're just sitting, Dad. Sometimes we just like to sit.' Their answer confused me a little, but then I realised I could learn from them. We are born pure and empty, the emptiness of being new. During our lives we are filled with experience but the purity gets lost. It's inevitable I suppose. Some of us, perhaps many of us, find it again. Experiences such as this climb bring us back to that emptiness, but it takes discipline to step beyond what we know and to leave the past behind. It's a form of enlightenment. I was just sitting there, waiting for the sun to transform snow into water. The paradise of my early youth was being regained. Reborn. I was alive and approaching some sort of Nirvana. I thought about life: how it all seems just to happen, how it was born out of chaos, from some greenish primordial gloop that surged through a fissure in the earth's crust to bubble to the surface. There is – must be – a spirit that sparked this chaos off. I remembered sitting by our month-old baby Hannah's cot. She had smiled at me as she woke, seeming to know full well that I had been looking into her relaxed face as she slept. Now, I was awake too and truly aware. These wonderings left me inspired. I realised that I was bursting to move and it was time to go.

I woke Rick, who was weak and rather lethargic. I encouraged him to change out of his clothes, reminding him that as we were much lower now and would probably be in the sun all day we could afford to shed some layers. At first he said he couldn't be bothered, but eventually found the energy to remove his harness and outer layers and then put his harness on again. While he was doing this, I heard movement somewhere below us, although we couldn't see anyone. I wondered if the porters Ali had sent around to the Diamir side had managed to climb up and meet us. But there was no sign of anyone and we decided that there must be people below us, probably climbing the fixed ropes on the Kinshofer Wall. I told Rick that I had managed to melt snow in our water bottles, and we shared a tiny sip of meltwater. It seemed to revive him.

We roped up again and Rick led off, with me following behind, still feeling strong enough to catch him if he fell. Although Rick was exhausted, I knew that he was a good and capable climber and so surefooted that even in this weakened state he was unlikely to slip. I trusted him, as he did me. We certainly couldn't afford to fall. After some awkward down-climbing and traversing we were about to climb down a steep slope that led to big rocks at the top of the Kinshofer Wall. These rocks were the anchors for the fixed ropes down it. At that moment we saw a man climbing upwards. He looked incredibly fit, clean and well-dressed in a black jacket with a huge logo printed on the arms. I called to him and he acknowledged us but kept moving a few more metres to clip himself into the top of the fixed ropes. He gave the impression of being very precise. Carefully, he attached himself to an anchor and then spoke to us. He was Czech, he said, and his English was poor. He looked amazed at seeing us, clearly wondering who we were and where we had come from. I immediately raised two fingers to my lips, as though putting a cigarette to my lips, the international symbol for: 'Can you give me a light?' Then I burrowed into my rucksack and dug out the Sumo stove. I held it up so he could see it and with my right hand mimed flicking a lighter with my thumb against the burner.

He understood immediately and from his rucksack pulled out a Thermos flask, unscrewed the top and handed a cup full of liquid to Rick. Rick was suddenly quiet and still, apparently reluctant to take the cup. It occurred to me that he was thinking that drinking from someone else's Thermos might undermine our alpine-style ascent. I said, 'Drink it, Rick. We're dying. You have to take some fluids.' He slugged it down and immediately vomited it all back up. The Czech climber realised this was a natural reaction for someone who had been out on a limb for a while and smiled nicely, took back the cup and refilled it, returning it to us both. He said in his broken English that his partner was coming and that he spoke better English. While he was speaking he handed me a small lighter.

I made a small shelf in the snow and set the stove up. It lit first time and immediately I began melting snow. The sound of the gas turning to flame and roaring under the pot warmed my very heart and sent shivers of relief right through my body. The Czech climber was trying to tell us his name – 'Marek!' – and signalled that he suspected we were 'the crazy Scottish guys on the Mazeno.' I had a huge grin on my face and laughed: 'Yep, that's us, but we are not crazy!' I didn't tell him that twelve hours earlier I'd been worrying about an imaginary rabbit's frozen paws.

It wasn't long before Marek's climbing companion, Zdeněk, arrived. He was much less strict about tying in and simply hung from his jumar while he spoke to us in good English. They both seemed blown away by seeing us and couldn't really believe we were descending their climb. They said things in Czech between themselves and then were rummaging inside their rucksacks before handing us a packet of glucose sweets. I tore the packet open with my teeth before passing a handful to Rick, telling him to get them down him. He was still very quiet, as though the enormity of meeting these two strangers was overwhelming him. I stuffed my share into my mouth and chewed happily. By this time the Sumo stove had melted water and I handed a mug of hot liquid to Rick. This time he sipped cautiously and managed to hold the liquid down. I took some too and then set the pot on the burner again. Marek and Zdeněk explained they were now the only team at Base Camp. The bad weather had dumped lots of snow on the mountain, making conditions hopelessly dangerous for the other teams. They told us that some of the commercially guided parties had reached Camp 2 but had judged conditions on the mountain so poor that they all abandoned their attempts and went home. We had, they implied, just spent three days ploughing down a gigantic avalanche zone.

Rick and I took in all this information. We had felt at times that conditions had indeed been dangerous and had triggered small avalanches ourselves. But things hadn't been quite that bad. Of course, there was a huge difference in commitment and difficulty between two alpinists on a new route and clients on commercial expeditions following established routes and using locals to fix a bannister of ropes up the mountain for their paying clients. It was the difference between my life as a high-altitude alpinist and my life as a mountain guide, with a duty of care to clients who want the adventure without so much of the risk. It's the difference between breaking free and calculating a compromise. Clients want someone else to judge the weather and snow conditions – to take responsibility for them, even while they enjoy the aura of the unpredictable nature you find in the mountains. If something does go wrong then lawyers often get involved to pursue the guide. No wonder everyone had gone home. But if people thought we'd been reckless, some of the answer lay in that choice – between taking risks for yourself and being paid to do it for someone else.

When I climb with my buddies I feel safe, because I know they can belay properly, look after themselves and be of solid assistance in risky climbing environments. Competence reduces the risk and so we climb harder things. When climbing with buddies who are also paying clients, things are different. Sometimes they struggle to belay efficiently, or misunderstand the terrain, or else don't move fast enough when things get difficult. These are risks too, just like avalanches or séracs, and as these risks increase, the scale of adventure gets turned down in response – there might be more fixed ropes and more porters, for example. This may come as a surprise to clients who have paid for the adventure of a lifetime on Everest or Mont Blanc, but commercial expeditions are a contradiction in terms. They're like the idyllic Alpine village that cashes in and builds a ski resort, turning a sanctuary into a zoo. Property prices skyrocket, the locals complain and the area loses its character.

While we sat wearily melting snow, the two Czechs introduced themselves properly as Marek Holeček and Zdeněk Hrubý. They were, they explained, on the Diamir side of Nanga Parbat to acclimatise for a new route they were hoping to climb on the Rupal Face. Like us, in our original planning at least, they had opted to climb up to Camp 2 on this side of the mountain to acclimatise and prepare themselves for their big adventure. I had read about Marek's exploits before; he's a well-known and very bold alpinist.

Zdeněk then said he thought we would definitely win the Piolets d'Or, world alpinism's equivalent to the Oscars. That amazed me. Up to that point I had never even considered any type of award for doing something I loved so much. I simply had wanted to climb the Mazeno for the love of the challenge; the idea of some golden trinket really disappointed me. But Rick agreed with them and said, 'Oh do you think so? That would be cool.' I realised then that I was climbing for very different reasons.

That same realisation had happened to me before, many years ago: Mal Duff and I decided that we were going to try and climb Lhotse Middle, which at that time was the highest unclimbed 8,000-metre summit in the world. To climb it, you had either to do the normal route on Lhotse and then traverse an incredibly technical knife-edge ridge, or climb to the South Col of Everest and head south into the wilds beyond, which was the route the Russians eventually took when they made the impressive first ascent in 2001. Both these routes included a wild traverse at over 8,000 metres and to me that was an exciting proposition.

Mal and I thought of a third way: we might be able to take a diagonal line across the south face of Lhotse, on to Lhotse Shar, and then traverse the ridge over to Lhotse Middle and continue along that sharp rocky ridge before descending via the normal route of Lhotse to Everest Base Camp. That would have been a truly cool new climb. It was without doubt terribly ambitious for the time. Of course it ended early on – about three quarters of the way up Lhotse Shar, Mal and I came to some incredibly difficult and steep ice up the side of unstable séracs. It was 8 a.m., we had been climbing all night and the sun was beginning to rise.

Ice conditions were degrading. As Mal was leading one very steep section, some ice broke off and hit Mal, splitting his head open and causing him to fall. I held him and lowered him off the steep wall. Together we wrapped his head in a stretchy crepe bandage and then, over a few days, I got him down to Base Camp. It was a bit of an epic descent but just part of one of the adventures that Mal and I had.

It was obvious Mal was no longer fit to climb, so with a BBC reporter, Iain Macwhirter, and our poet friend Andrew Greig, Mal walked out to Lukla and flew home. While going through Kathmandu he visited the Ministry of Tourism, which had granted us our climbing permits, and it decided that our attempt would be abandoned as only I was left on the mountain. Of course there were no easy communications in those days so I had no knowledge Mal had done this. I was fit as a fiddle and decided to hang out at Base Camp, getting in touch with my friends Jeff Lowe, Mark Twight and Alison Hargreaves. Alison and Jeff had just climbed a new route on Kantega and Jeff was about to start a new climb on Nuptse with the very young and very likable Mark.

I spent a bit of time hanging out with them in Jeff's famous base camp tent where he had a big inflatable armchair sat comfortably in the centre of a fine Tibetan carpet. Alison was due to go home but I convinced her to come climbing with me on Lhotse Shar. So with Jeff's help and that of the expedition's liaison officer, we wrote to the Ministry of Tourism asking that as Mal Duff was injured, would the Ministry consider adding Miss Alison Hargreaves to our permit so that our new team could try our climb again? We sent a Sherpa running back to Kathmandu with the letter.

The weather was good in the mountains so Alison and I teamed up and headed back up to my own simple base camp. We got back up to our previous high point, where we established ourselves in a snow cave at around 6,800 metres. That night a big storm came in and we were stuck in the snow cave for a few days. Once the weather cleared Alison and I decided to push on up the mountain, but the slopes above were so loaded with unstable snow that the avalanche risk was simply too great. We decided to go down and give the snow a few days to settle. I remember feeling very at ease with Alison, thinking she was cool, capable and together. As we abseiled down, still several hundred metres above our base camp, we could see below, in the far distance, lots of people milling around and we wondered what was going on down there. We actually thought that a trekking group must be passing by and we looked forward to sharing tea with them and hoped that we would get some up-to-date news and banter.

As we got closer we realised the people were in military uniforms and when we arrived in camp, knackered and exhausted after our climb, they told us we were climbing without permission and arrested me. I could not believe it. But I had to pack up my gear and was escorted in military fashion all the way to Namche Bazaar, where I had to spend the night in their rudimentary police lock-up drinking copious amounts of tea with the friendly policeman. I was accompanied by military police on the flight to Kathmandu and then taken to the Ministry. There I was interviewed by men in uniforms and I explained everything with all my best Scottish Highland charm; I could not really understand why I was in such dreadful trouble. I had climbed in Nepal for many years and over that time had established a good reputation as an honest enough fellow. I was told that I had to stay in a hotel in Kathmandu and that a military presence was to be posted at the hotel. I was under a form of house arrest. I had to give the military time to discuss my situation.

I had of course apologised profusely and continued to explain my side of the story and my innocence. Thanks to Jeff Lowe, his Sherpas and my own Nepali agent who all played their part, I was finally cleared. I remain grateful for their assistance. Eventually the Ministry escorted me back to their offices and they explained that Mal had visited and told them to close the expedition. Even with a head injury I thought he had more sense than to hand back a climbing permit with someone still on the mountain. Once I got back to Scotland I telephoned him but he couldn't come up with a satisfactory explanation and admitted he only wanted to try Lhotse Middle to enhance his guiding reputation.

I was so upset and disappointed that we just drifted apart and I did not climb with him again. Eventually, after ten years or so, we became friends again as we bumped into each other while guiding clients on winter climbs on Ben Nevis. I ended up guiding for Mal on Cho Oyu and while I was there we received the terrible news that he had suffered a fatal heart attack at Everest Base Camp. I was so sad hearing of Mal's death; I realised we had been incredibly good friends for an important phase of our lives and had shared some good climbing. Thanks to Mal I had been able to live out some amazing dreams and adventures. He was a rough diamond indeed.

We said our goodbyes to the Czech team, thanking them profusely. They continued upwards, as they were heading to Camp 2 where they planned to bivvy for the night. Sleeping at that altitude would aid their acclimatisation in preparation for their planned new route on the Rupal Face. As he went, Marek shouted back down to us to help ourselves to their tent and food at Camp 1. I shouted my thanks and handed Rick the pot of warmed snow melt. We shared the remaining liquid and then I packed the stove carefully into my sack and we set off down to the top of the fixed ropes.

11

RETURN

Once I'd clipped into the tangle of old fixed ropes leading down the Kinshofer Wall I belayed Rick as he abseiled down. When he was down fifty metres, I followed behind. I soon realised that the old ropes were just too worn and tight to allow a safe and efficient descent. With little discussion we decided to abseil using our own rope. It was back to the hassle of short abseils. I threaded the rope through the best anchors I could find and abseiled down first. Once I was clipped in, I held the ends of our rope as Rick followed. I watched him painfully clip and unclip from the ropes, his fingers still half-frozen and his mind exhausted. Once he was off the abseil ropes, I quickly pulled them through, re-threaded them and set the next abseil while Rick caught his breath. Once I was down, I shouted up and we repeated the process, again and again, until finally we reached the bottom. Here we found a mass of old ropes, twisted pitons and abandoned electron ladders. The standard routes on 8,000-metre peaks are filling up with this detritus.

Once on the snow we roped up again. I went to the back with the bulk of the rope stowed away in my sack and let Rick climb down in front of me. My hallucinations had ended as the air thickened. My deep exhaustion had eased with liquid and a little food inside me. I felt euphoric but knew this feeling wouldn't last long. I wanted to keep pushing on down. Rick was still very weak and I could tell from the way he moved and kicked in his feet that his toes were frozen hard. He simply didn't have the energy to move any faster.

We were at the top of a broad couloir pitched at about forty or fifty degrees. This had not been a big deal the last time we were here when it was fixed with lots of rope and had footsteps up it. This time there was none of that. It consisted of a thin layer of snow with dark grey ice underneath that was as hard as rock. If we kicked hard with our crampon points they simply bounced off. We had to climb it very carefully and delicately. My old Czech ice axe was by this time totally blunt after all the mixed climbing we had done and I felt very precarious down-climbing it for myself, let alone trying to offer a tight rope to a battle-weary Rick.

After we'd gone about a hundred metres, Rick said: 'Sandy, I just have to stop, I am exhausted.' For Rick to say this out loud was exceptional; even in the middle of our trials higher up the mountain he hadn't uttered a word of complaint. Normally he never admitted to any sort of weakness. We stopped for about ten minutes and as we rested I reminded us both that if we could get down this couloir in an hour then we should be back at camp before darkness. We continued our descent. The route took a curving arc to the other side of the couloir and then went straight down, with me climbing directly above Rick. The snow fell intermittently and in a way we were lucky we were not exposed to hot sunshine. Even so, the avalanche risk from above preyed on our minds and we knew that the faster we got down the couloir the faster we'd be out of the line of fire.

We had probably six metres of rope out between us, but I kept some coils in one hand as we climbed down, facing into the slope. Rick at least had two ice tools. Our toes were frozen, Rick's worse than mine. His hands were also cold as his mittens had frozen solid. I wouldn't go so far as to say that the Czech team saved us from death, but the water they gave us and the packet of glucose sweets – as well as a Snickers bar Marek handed us – meant we had the strength to climb more safely. It was also good that we could move together rather than having to pitch the whole thing. I felt much more secure protecting my buddy when I was directly above him, but knew at the same time that if he fell off, it would be hard for me to stop any kind of fall. I was also aware that I simply could not afford to make a mistake, despite the pain in my feet. If I fell, that would be it for both of us.

Rick kept asking for more and more stops, and to protect my friend I wasn't going to say no. But each time I would count the seconds as they turned into minutes. On several occasions Rick fell completely asleep as he climbed and I had to be ready to hold a fall. It became quite unnerving, although the hours passed in a flash. Darkness came, and we were still only three-quarters of the way down the couloir. I could not believe how long it was taking, but I dug deep inside myself and said a prayer asking God to give me the patience to stay cool, and to give us both the strength to keep on keeping on. I don't think I would have travelled much faster if we had decided to down-climb unroped. My feet had become progressively more painful and I had to stifle little gasps of pain each time I kicked my front points in slightly too hard. I didn't want Rick to feel less than totally secure; if I just stayed calm and patient and continued acting as a reliable companion then he would not get frustrated with his own exhaustion. We were slow, but we kept a steady rhythm and that helped.

A very loud voice shouted up at us from below. I assumed this roaring from the depths must be one of our Pakistani porters. I hoped beyond hope it was, and that, although they were unskilled at climbing, they had maybe come up to Camp 1. I hadn't expected any help above this point. They would need crampons and ice axes and it was unlikely they had those. I saw a flash of light dance briefly across the slope. 'Hey, there is at least one person below us around the site of Camp 1,' I said to Rick.

He agreed and we decided it was probably Ali's porters, but could not quite work out how they had managed to get to Camp 1 so quickly. It was only a couple of days or so since we'd called Ali. All went silent again. There was no more shouting or flashing of lights and we continued on our downward climb. Whoever was below had gone quiet and I think we both wondered if we were imagining the voice and the light. Were we hallucinating again?

Rick called for another stop and this time I said no, trying to reason with him: 'Let's get going, Rick. We have to get off here; it's getting really dark. If we stop we'll need more clothes and it's just too precarious on this slope.' He ignored me and came to a halt. 'I have to stop.' So I thumped in the dulled pick of my ice axe and clove-hitched the rope to it while keeping the rope between us tight. I tried to ease my feet into some sort of restful state, one at a time, to take the pressure off my semi-frozen toes. I mentioned my pain to Rick, who replied that I was lucky: 'Mine have been dead for days.'

Then he fell soundly asleep again and I decided I should simply let it happen.

I counted ten minutes, silently ticking off the seconds, all the way to sixty, ten times, bending one finger at a time inside my mittens to keep count as I reached the end of each estimated minute. After that I gently called to him to wake up.

'Did I nod off?' he asked.

'Oh just a bit.'

I told him I was cooling down and put on another layer. 'How about you?' He simply stood up and continued on downwards. As we approached the apron at the foot of the couloir we were able to turn outwards and walk, albeit carefully and on a very steep slope. I stopped and suggested we got our head torches out, which took a while. Moving on again, I noted that Rick was moving faster now. He seemed to sense where we were and was making a concerted dash for Camp 1, which was still some distance away. It lay hidden from above, tucked into the lee of a rock spur which protected the camp from the regular avalanches that slid most days down the couloir we had just descended.

In the dark I could see the bergschrund, which didn't seem too bad; a tumble of avalanche debris had filled the gap and frozen over, leaving only the occasional deep black hole. Soon afterwards we crossed it and came to Camp 1. As soon as we saw it we shouted. Soon figures were rushing out of a small cluster of tents – it was the porters Ali had sent, switching their head torches on to give each one a bright shining eye, like the Cyclops. We climbed up the gentle slope towards them and shook their hands, greeting one another like long-lost friends. They were genuinely pleased to see us. The Pakistani people from these areas are renowned for their wildness, but these men had an amazing respect for us and were delighted to help in any way they could. I loved these guys, had known some of them since my early days climbing Muztagh Tower and had an understanding of their tough, no-nonsense approach to life. They've endured shattering earthquakes and flooding, while competing Shi'ite and Sunni Muslims have been fighting for centuries, taking pot shots at each other across their rough fields. Men who had portered for us in the 1980s were now village elders and had told stories to their sons and grandsons who now stood before us.

There is no doubt that many of these mountain people are sometimes exploited by some of the larger trekking-company bosses who sit in offices in Islamabad and Rawalpindi. Even though Western climbers pay high fees for porter wages, it doesn't always all get passed on to them. Happily, thanks to our excellent agent, our guys weren't in that position and when we needed them they were truly loyal to the core. Our plight crossed all boundaries; we were all of us mountain people. I have found this to be true across the mountain regions of the world. A dam burst inside me, and I was engulfed by a flood of relief as the tension of the past weeks lifted for the first time. I wondered how the porters had managed to get all the way to Camp 1 from Skardu in such a short time and we let them tell their story as we drank the hot soup they had prepared for us. They had, they said, driven overnight and marched up here in a continuous forty-eight-hour push from Skardu. I thanked them from the bottom of my heart.

They rushed around and fed us more hot soup. There were water biscuits with local cheese and lots of sweet biscuits. Rick and I gobbled up the food; it didn't touch the sides as I swallowed it all. The porters were amazed at the speed we ate and drank and realised they had to get more snow melted, apologising that they had no more food for us. They had rushed up here very quickly and only brought a small amount. They were glad to see us alive and it slowly dawned on me that they half-expected to be ferrying our corpses to the roadhead.

We were all tired, but Rick and I needed to sleep immediately. I let them then know that Marek the Czech climber said we could use their tent, so with lots of good nights and expressions of deep gratitude, we bid each and every one a good night. Rick crawled into his own tent and I into Marek's. Within minutes I had to crawl out again to pass a tiny amount of urine; it was greenish and stung me as the liquid came out but I was delighted and relieved to know I could still pee. I went down to where the porters were camped and asked through their partly zipped tent door if there was any water. They selflessly poured some of theirs into my water bottle. I appreciated everything they did; their presence was vital to me and I no longer felt the weight of responsibility on my shoulders. I stumbled to the tent, taking one last look around camp in the darkness. It was hauntingly beautiful and I felt so alive. I ducked into the tent, pulled my sleeping bag from my sack, noting that it felt damp. Then I saw a yellow sleeping bag. It must have been Marek's and seemed enticingly dry and fluffed up, so, thanking him very much under my breath, I sat on it, undid the Velcro of my gaiters and kicked off my boots. My feet were finally free of their prison. Even now, after everything I'd been through, I found myself fastidiously knocking the dirt off the soles and storing them carefully inside the tent. I half zipped the tent flap, slipped off my socks and climbed into Marek's wonderfully dry bag.

Sleep engulfed me.

When I was woken by the noise of the porters moving around outside, it was still dark. Oh bugger, I thought, what are they are up to? All I wanted to do was lie there. There was a clattering of pots and as I unzipped the tent to investigate I saw Rick was already dressed and up.

'Come on, Sandy,' he said, 'we have to go. They're worried about the glacier and séracs; we should get out of here while it's still frozen.' One of the porters thrust a jug of tea into my hand. I drank the tea and munched on a handful of biscuits before tidying up the tent. We left for Base Camp wearing crampons but soon came to bare glacier ice that was smothered in small moraine grit and pebbles, so after weaving through an area of exposed crevasses we were able to take them off and walk more freely. We did not need or use the rope.

I took photos looking up at the Mummery Rib and felt suddenly a huge sadness. The mist was down and the Mazeno was hidden from view. I remembered looking at old black and white photos of Fred Mummery and his Gurkhas. We had finally fulfilled his dream and put a British route up Nanga Parbat, more than a hundred years after he died trying. I thought too of Günther Messner and said a quick prayer, thanking God for our good luck and his protection, our lives, our skills and our porters, Cathy and the three Lhakpas. As we walked on I said to Rick: 'We've done it, you know.' He punched me in the friendly way that men often do, acknowledging our luck and achievement. I think there were tears welling in his eyes but he said nothing. My feet were sore and Rick hobbled along.

As we came to the edge of the glacier, Samandar, Muhammad Hussain and the cook boys met us. I felt myself grinning from ear to ear. They stopped in front of me and ceremoniously placed a garland of flowers over my head and rested it gently on my neck and shoulders. We shook hands, I said my thanks and immediately apologised for being such a softie. 'It's fantastic to see you all, I cannot thank you enough.' Rick had garlands of flowers too and we posed for photographs. They shook our hands and rubbed my hatted head, patted my shoulders and were so delighted to be part of this amazing expedition. Samandar said he thought we might have died but he always knew in his heart of hearts that Rick and I would not die in the mountains. He said: 'You are the strongest climbers, maybe the strongest of all.' A wave of humility caught me; I loved these Pakistani high-mountain people but could say nothing, overwhelmed with emotion. Seeking some form of composure I buried my face in his shoulder thanking him and his team for all their help.

We moved on, the Pakistani team insisting on taking our rucksacks. I did not wish to relinquish mine but eventually, with all their pleading, I succumbed and let them help; they wished to be involved. The glacier ended and after just a short section of moraine the path climbed steeply up to the grassy plain and moraine ridges which brought us to Base Camp. A vast carpet of colourful wild flowers greeted us and we walked on slowly, soon coming to the Czech base camp. Two big mess tents, one for cooking and the other for dining, were surrounded with various smaller tents for the climbers and Pakistani support team to sleep in.

Someone rushed over two plastic chairs for Rick and me to sit in. I suddenly couldn't cope with this, and weaved away to sit on a big rock adjacent to the cook tent. I had sat on this rock many times in the past, chatting to various climbing friends from all over the world. Now I had it to myself. Someone brought me a big mug of tea as I kicked my boots off and peeled off my filthy socks to reveal my feet. My toes were white, but a delicate off-white that wasn't too alarming. Every nail was numb but looked okay, apart from my big toe on my right foot, which was numb and pearly white. I sensed that while damaged it would eventually be okay.

I sat against the rock, looking over to Rick in his plastic chair and watching the Czech climbers and our porters as they sat outside the cook tent drinking tea and talking about events. It was a special moment. The Pakistani people were saying how amazing it was that we were here, alive. It was unbelievable to them that we had been at such altitudes for so long. That we had traversed the Mazeno to the summit and come back alive. I drank the rest of my tea and enjoyed the sensation of walking on the grass in my bare feet to join Rick in the chairs.

A friendly Czech wanted to administer an injection to Rick to kick-start his circulation and prevent further cold injury to his fingers and feet. They offered me some and pointing to my toes I said I would be fine. I asked them if they had any antibiotics and they came back with a blister pack. Then Rick and I sat there while they took photos and we drank our tea on the grassy terrace facing the Diamir Face of Nanga Parbat. The sun shone brightly, dazzlingly white against the snow, and I wondered how it was that this killer mountain had let us off after such a protracted ordeal. There was a crashing sound as the first sérac of the day fell from the mountain. Nanga Parbat was waking up. Soon the noise of thundering avalanches would echo around the valley. Miles below the plastic chair I rested on, tectonic plates shifted slowly, as they have for millions of years, thrusting Nanga Parbat higher into the air, letting the summit scratch the belly of the clouds above. The hanging glaciers and séracs cracked and groaned as the mountain heaved and flexed, pulsing like a living thing. The world turned. And in all this movement I could not feel the slightest breath of wind upon my face.

Seventeen years since we first attempted the Mazeno Ridge with Doug Scott, Voytek Kurtyka and Andrew Lock, for some inexplicable reason, my buddy Rick and I had been permitted to make this first ascent. The rest of our team, Cathy, Rangdu, Zarok and Nuru, were waiting for us at the hotel in Chilas. It had been eighteen days since we left Base Camp on the Rupal side to attempt the monstrous, inescapable ridge. We had shared some amazing climbing along this knife-edged, corniced ridge on the ninth-highest summit in the world. We had committed to the impossible, breathed the rarest air and shared bonds of unlimited human effort. We had been blessed with kindness.

I swallowed my cup of tea, exchanging ideas with Samandar about how we could thank the Czechs for their wonderful camaraderie. He rushed away to share our ideas with the expedition cooks. A runner was immediately dispatched with a handful of currency to buy supplies. He headed down the valley towards a nearby village where local people farmed in isolated simplicity, herding flocks of goats and sheep and nurturing crops in the thin soil.

Rick and I hung our sleeping bags over a tent and took a short nap, but I soon woke again and just sat there, drinking tea and eating, eating, eating. In the middle of the afternoon Marek and Zdeněk returned from their acclimatisation trip to Camp 2. By evening we had all washed and were sharing a Czech beer or three. The cook brought us plates of newly purchased goat meat cooked in a variety of simple but tasty curried sauces with vegetables pulled straight from the soil, deliciously fresh as a spring morning. The evening passed away in the briefest flash, hours reduced to mere minutes.

Semi-inebriated and overflowing with food I staggered to my tent in the small hours. The cooks and staff had all gone to their respective sleeping places. Surrounded by silence, Marek and I snuffed out the last candles. Above our heads the diamond stars studded the heavens, lighting the proud summit of Nanga Parbat. Forcing myself to turn away from its majestic, gigantic splendour, I crawled into my sleeping bag and lay my head to sleep.

We had done it, and come back.

Life was the sweetest thing.

ACKNOWLEDGEMENTS

Thanks to my family, and to the many climbers who have helped me over the years and become close friends along the way – you know who you are! Thanks in particular to Douglas Scott CBE for introducing me to the Mazeno Ridge and so many other mountaineering adventures.

I must thank Rick Allen for his friendship and another great climb. And Cathy O'Dowd, Lhakpa Rangdu Sherpa, Lhakpa Nuru Sherpa and Lakpa Zarok Sherpa, without whose help, loyalty, determination and camaraderie we would have never reached the summit. My thanks to Muhammad Ali and all his staff who were so professional, efficient and acted so swiftly – and some of whom travelled a huge distance on foot through the night to meet us at the Kinshofer Camp 1. And Marek Holeček and the late Zdeněk Hrubý and their base camp team for the drinks, lighter, snacks and dry sleeping bags and friendship. Thanks to Voytek Kurtyka for talking and understanding what it's like to live such an adventure, and for helping me to open up and find confidence to talk about my hallucinations.

Helen O'Neill, Dr Eunice Atkins, Andrew Greig and Gabriela Kühn for their encouragement. Thanks also to Andrew for permission to reproduce an excerpt from his poem 'Three Above Namche Bazaar'.

Thanks to the Mount Everest Foundation and the British Mountaineering Council, and Mountain Equipment and PHD design.

Thanks to Cathy, Rick and Rangdu for taking such great photos which help to illustrate the story of our climb, and also to those climbers and friends who have supplied additional photographs for this book: Steve Razzetti, Markus Walter, Jochen Hemmleb, Robert Schauer, Doug Chabot and Pascal Tournaire.

And finally to Ed Douglas, my editor, and all at Vertebrate Publishing especially John Coefield, Nathan Ryder and Jane Beagley for taking the chance and for their outstanding work and attention to detail. It's been an amazing experience.

ABOUT THE AUTHOR

© www.norbert-freudenthaler.com

Sandy Allan was born and raised in Dalwhinnie in the Highlands of Scotland, and has been climbing since his teens. During the 1980s and 1990s he established many hard new winter and mixed climbs in Scotland, and he continues to be an active climber and new route developer.

He is an IFMGA/UIAGM mountain guide and has guided clients to the summits of many of the highest mountains in the world, including Mount Everest, Cho Oyu and Nanga Parbat. As well as guiding in the Himalaya, Sandy has been involved in many expeditions, including the Muztagh Tower, Lhotse West and the Scottish Direct Route on the south face of Pumori. In 2012, over the course of eighteen days and in alpine style, he and his partner Rick Allen completed the first ascent of one of the Himalaya's most coveted unclimbed lines – the Mazeno Ridge of Nanga Parbat. In recognition of their ascent, Rick and Sandy were awarded the 2013 Piolet d'Or.

INDEX

01 (L–R) Gregor, William, me, Mum, Eunice and Max. Photo: Sandy Allan collection.

02 Me and Greg hillwalking in the Cairngorms. Photo: Sandy Allan collection.

03 Me climbing on the early part of the Mazeno Ridge on Doug Scott's 1995 expedition. Photo: Rick Allen.

04 Voytek Kurtyka close to the 'point of no return' during our attempt on the Mazeno in 1995. Photo: Rick Allen.

05 Lhakpa Rangdu Sherpa, Lakpa Zarok Sherpa and Lhakpa Nuru Sherpa at Tarshing. Photo: Sandy Allan.
06 Me on the left with Cathy and Rick at Tarshing. Photo: Sandy Allan collection.

NANGA PARBAT
(8,126 METRES)

MAZENO RIDGE

RUPAL (TOSHAINI) GLACIER

07 The Mazeno Ridge, with the key features highlighted: Base Camp, our bivvy sites along the ridge,
    the Mazeno Gap, and the descent route taken by Cathy, Rangdu, Zarok and Nuru. Photo: Markus Walter.

08 Breaking trail along the ridge, shortly before Nuru's fall. Photo: Rick Allen.

09 Zarok and Nuru at our forced bivvy, after Nuru's fall. Photo: Lhakpa Rangdu.

10 Rick pictured at the 'point of no return'. Photo: Sandy Allan.

11 (L–R) Nuru, Zarok and Cathy pick their way through unstable terrain. Photo: Lhakpa Rangdu.

12 Me breaking trail on the traverse of the Diamir west flank, the day before we summited. Photo: Rick Allen.

13 Looking back along the ridge from the Diamir west flank. Photo: Sandy Allan.

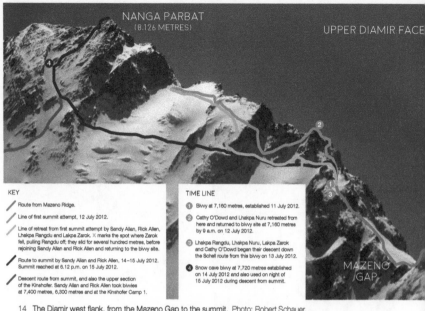

NANGA PARBAT
(8,126 METRES)

UPPER DIAMIR FACE

KEY

Route from Mazeno Ridge.

Line of first summit attempt, 12 July 2012.

Line of retreat from first summit attempt by Sandy Allan, Rick Allen, Lhakpa Rangdu and Lakpa Zarok. X marks the spot where Zarok fell, pulling Rangdu off; they slid for several hundred metres, before rejoining Sandy Allan and Rick Allen and returning to the bivvy site.

Route to summit by Sandy Allan and Rick Allen, 14–15 July 2012. Summit reached at 6.12 p.m. on 15 July 2012.

Descent route from summit, and also the upper section of the Kinshofer. Sandy Allan and Rick Allen took bivvies at 7,400 metres, 6,300 metres and at the Kinshofer Camp 1.

TIME LINE

① Bivvy at 7,160 metres, established 11 July 2012.

② Cathy O'Dowd and Lhakpa Nuru retreated from here and returned to bivvy site at 7,160 metres by 9 a.m. on 12 July 2012.

③ Lhakpa Rangdu, Lhakpa Nuru, Lakpa Zarok and Cathy O'Dowd began their descent down the Schell route from this bivvy on 13 July 2012.

④ Snow cave bivvy at 7,720 metres established on 14 July 2012 and also used on night of 15 July 2012 during descent from summit.

MAZENO
GAP

14 The Diamir west flank, from the Mazeno Gap to the summit. Photo: Robert Schauer.

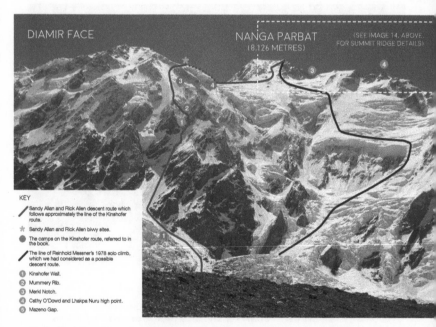

DIAMIR FACE

NANGA PARBAT
(8,126 METRES)

(SEE IMAGE 14, ABOVE,
FOR SUMMIT RIDGE DETAILS)

KEY

Sandy Allan and Rick Allen descent route which follows approximately the line of the Kinshofer route.

★ Sandy Allan and Rick Allen bivvy sites.

● The camps on the Kinshofer route, referred to in the book.

The line of Reinhold Messner's 1978 solo climb, which we had considered as a possible descent route.

① Kinshofer Wall.

② Mummery Rib.

③ Merkl Notch.

④ Cathy O'Dowd and Lhakpa Nuru high point.

⑤ Mazeno Gap.

15 The Diamir Face of Nanga Parbat, showing the line of our descent. Photo: J. Hemmleb, Lana (Italy).

16   Rick, feeling the effects of almost two weeks' climbing. The Diamir glacier in the distance.
          Photo: Sandy Allan.

17–18 Czech climbers Marek Holeček (left) and Zdeněk Hrubý (right), who were so kind to us at the
          top of the Kinshofer Wall. Photos: Sandy Allan.

19 A good cup of tea at the Kinshofer Base Camp, thanks to the generosity of the Czechs. Photo: Sandy Allan.
20 Me and Rick in Chamonix, 2013. Photo: Pascal Tournaire.

Lightning Source UK Ltd.
Milton Keynes UK
UKHW040723110820
368048UK00002B/386